# Philosophy Fridays

## Armchair Philosophy Sessions from a High School Physics Teacher

### Matt D'Antuono

En Route Books & Media, LLC
St. Louis, MO

En Route Books and Media, LLC
5705 Rhodes Avenue
St. Louis, MO 63109

Cover credit: TJ Burdick

Library of Congress Control Number:
2019943236

ISBN-13: 978-1-950108-10-7
ISBN-10: 1-950108-10-4

# Dedication

For my students, who began Philosophy Friday and without whom this book would have been much, much, much harder to write.

# Acknowledgments

I must begin, of course, by thanking my students for their curiosity about philosophy. I hope that their curiosity continues! Their feedback encouraged me to think about writing this book in the first place.

Thank you to my wife who read this book, corrected my typos, and gave me many suggestions for making the content clearer for readers.

Thank you to Stephen Barr for his work *Modern Physics, Ancient Faith,* from which I have many quotes on my wall, and for offering encouragement and helpful suggestions for this book.

Thank you to Sebastian Mahfood for all of his help in the publishing process.

# Table of contents

# 1. Introduction

While discussing the nature of science with my physics students a few years ago, I pointed out that our topic of conversation was technically not science anymore. Instead, when we are talking about the nature of science, we are doing philosophy. The rest of the conversation went something like this:

"What is philosophy? What is it about? How do you know about philosophy?"

"I have a degree in philosophy."

"But you teach physics. I thought you had a degree in physics."

"I do, but I also went back and got a second bachelor's degree in philosophy."

"You should teach us some philosophy."

I thought about that request, and I decided that it was a good idea. So, I began to start off class from time to time with a philosophical quote, dilemma, situation or conversation. At first, I stuck mainly to the philosophy of science since it was a physics class. But I got a little braver over time and moved on to the other topics in philosophy.

I was irregular with my philosophy class-starters. Sometimes I would do a few in a row, and then I started to run out of time for our unit of physics, so I wouldn't do one for a while. Eventually, my students and I decided that we should begin each Friday with some philosophy, and Philosophy Friday was born.

When students ask me to write a college recommendation for them, I ask them to tell me something from the class that

1

they remember so that I can get ideas about what to write. This year, I wrote over 20 college recommendations, and every student mentioned Philosophy Friday. Whenever my students write me a thank you card, they mention Philosophy Friday. Students come into class on Friday excited about Philosophy Friday. I have been told that Philosophy Friday helped students to start thinking differently about their lives. I have even had students from the previous year come in at the beginning of their free period on a Friday to relive Philosophy Friday. The feedback has been overwhelming. "Definitely, never stop Philosophy Friday," a graduating senior recently told me.

This book is an attempt to bring Philosophy Friday to a wider audience. Since you are not sitting in my classroom with a group of high school students, we cannot really recreate what happens during that time. Every class is different, and the conversation is never the same. Some classes are quieter so that I have to do more prompting; other classes need little help to get a raging discussion going. In an effort to render these conversations truthfully, I recorded Philosophy Friday in each of my classes one year, and much of this book is taken directly from those recordings, some from one class, some from another. I have had to leave out some of the honest but important questions that are frequently asked, like "Will this be on the test?" "Can I go to the bathroom?" and "How much do you bench?" Sometimes I do a lot of talking. Sometimes I do hardly any talking. Many times, students leave frustrated because I will not "just give them the right answer." Sometimes I feel badly because my own search for truth has led me to satisfying, rational answers to a lot of these questions, but these little sessions are not about me convincing them of my beliefs. Since I teach in a public school, that would probably get me fired, too. I will tell you, the reader, what I tell my students: if you want to learn what I believe and how I answer these questions, you can read my other books or visit my YouTube channel, DonecRequiescat. During these Philosophy Friday sessions, my goal is to challenge and inspire my students to think deeply about the tough but important and foundational questions in life.

The only time I don't do Philosophy Friday on a last-class-of-the-week is the day before some extended break. On those days, I conduct a "freakin'-awesome-physics-Friday" talk. Since a normal class is usually worthless on those days (who can concentrate and learn productively the day before spring break?), I have my students sit back, relax, and listen to some of the things that blow my mind about physics and math like relativity, black holes, astronomy and astrophysics, transfinite numbers and set theory, and then, on the last day of class, the beauty of physics. Since this book is about philosophy, I have decided to only include the final lecture on beauty and physics because it is the synthesis of physics and philosophy and the culmination of the course. (By the way, for any of my fellow teachers out there, I highly recommend using your days-before-breaks this way. Just tell your students about some of the things that blow your mind about your subject. Let them know what you love about what you teach.)

I have also included part of my first lecture because that is the day I tell them about Philosophy Friday and we do our first philosophical reflection.

I have taken almost all of my questions and ideas from other sources. *The Book of Questions* by Gregory Stock has been a helpful resource for good "life-choice" dilemmas. Other questions and passages come from a variety of philosophical sources, and I usually give credit where I can. I am sure, though, that I have internalized and continued to use questions and ideas from other sources, which I have forgotten. For that reason, I doubt that there is a single original idea in this text. Thankfully, that is not the goal.

To those readers who are educated in philosophy, I beg your pardon for not using technical terminology and sticking to strictly precise explanations. I find it best when introducing a new subject to avoid all jargon. I do introduce some terms just to give the students a taste of the dialect, but I don't carry on the conversation with those words. This is philosophy in broad strokes. Detail comes with time and experience, and while I hope my students may come to know and appreciate the finer points and distinctions, they are still a long way off.

You may find that there are a lot of "life situations" and tough decision questions, especially in the beginning. Philosophically, they relate primarily to ethics and philosophical anthropology, but I find them to be the most relatable questions and topics for my students. While I have a few metaphysical questions thrown in at the beginning, it is a little tough to pull people in by starting off with the nature of existence of things. In the end, all of philosophy ties back to metaphysics, and I try to bring that out in the conversations.

The best way to join my class for Philosophy Fridays is to imagine yourself as a high school student. Picture yourself walking through the hallways on a Friday. It has been a busy week, like always. The pressures of tests, quizzes, homework, sports, clubs, nagging teachers, annoying classmates, friends, and everything else are almost at an end for the week. Some people are rude. Some are loud. Some smell bad. After walking up the stairs, the person who went ahead of you through the doorway doesn't hold the door open. It nearly slams you in the face. You see a friend in the hallway, but you already said hello to that friend, and you don't know whether to say hello again or not. It's awkward. You just keep your head down. You walk into your physics class. You take a seat at your table, which is a group of four desks put together, turn to your friend and ask what you are doing today.

"It's Friday!"

"I know. But what are we doing today?"

"It's Philosophy Friday!"

"Oh! Right!"

# 2. Why School?

*On the first day of school I take some time to introduce myself and tell them some of the details they need to know about grades and class materials they need to have. Then I try to spend some time provoking their thinking about school in the first place.*

Each Friday we are going to do something that has become a tradition in my class. A number of years ago some of my students found out that, besides my degree in physics, I have a degree in philosophy, too. They wanted me to teach them some philosophy, and I said ok. So, it turned into a tradition that we start off each class on Friday with Philosophy Friday. I hope that is ok with you. I have gotten a lot of positive feedback on it over the years.

Even though today is not Friday, we are still going to do a little philosophy. I think this is an important question. I want you to tell me why you are here in my classroom right now.

*The students are always shy on their first day.*

Did you wake up this morning and think to yourself, "Today I want to learn physics," so you found a school and looked up the schedule to show up in this room at this time?

"No."

No, I didn't think so.

Let's start with a broader question. Why did you come to school today?

"Because we had to."

That's right. You had to. But not if you are sixteen years old. You can drop out when you are sixteen.

"Then my parents would kill me."

*Laughter.*

"No, seriously. They would."

I am sorry to hear that. But let's think about why you should go to school. Do you think it's a good thing or not?

*Nods*

Why?

"Because we have to get into college."

Why go to college?

"So that we can get a good job."

Why get a good job?

"So that you can make a lot of money."

Why make a lot of money?

*Students are wondering about my sanity.*

"Because you need money to live and support a family and stuff."

Not necessarily. You need food and shelter and clothing, but you can steal all that stuff.

"Yeah, but if you do, then you'll get in trouble."

Ok. So, you are saying you should go to school so you can get into college, get a good job, make a lot of money, and have stuff. Why have stuff? I know some people who are homeless or poor, and they are living. Some have even chosen to live that way.

*At this point students are usually without an answer.*

Since you spend so much of your time in school, it is important to think about it to see if it is really worth your time.

Honestly, I think all of that is an important part of going to school, but I think there are more important reasons. First, though, I want to go back to a previous question. Why study physics?

"It's a graduation requirement."

True. So, see all of the above about college and money and stuff?

*Nods.*

Fair enough.

I want to show you a video clip, and then we are going to talk about why you should go to school and study physics.

*At this point I show the students a clip of Einstein the parrot doing some tricks and making a lot of fascinating sounds.*

Is that a smart bird?

*Nods.*

Is that a smart animal?

"Yeah"

We would say that is a smart animal, right? He can do a lot of stuff. But let me tell you something. Compared to what you can do, that bird is nothing. That bird has been trained. You can learn. There is an essential difference. Did you notice what the trainer was doing with her right hand? The microphone was in the left hand, but every now and then she gave a treat to the bird. Everything that bird does is stimulus and response. And that is true for everything every other animal does. It can be accounted for as stimulus and response. But you have been doing something today that no other animal on the planet can do as far as we know: you have been having conversations. You have been discussing your summer, what classes you have, what you have heard about your teachers from other students, and who knows what else. You can read words on a page. You can do arithmetic. You can compose a poem, even if it's a bad one. You can actually understand something.

Here is another thing you can do that no other animal can. Close your eyes. Picture in your mind a mountain. Got it? Now, make it a mountain of gold. You are imagining something you have never seen by combining two things you have seen in your mind. No other animal can do that. Do some animals have amazing abilities? Yes. But none other has a rational mind.

The most important reason to go to school is to develop this essential part of yourself to be the very best that it can be. You should go to school to train your mind, and that is more important, as far as I am concerned, than making money.

As I hope you come to see as the year goes on, I ask a lot of questions, and I try not to do something or believe something unless I have good reason to. So I wouldn't be a teacher unless I thought it was really important.

Physics is a particular habit of mind. It is not the only way to train your mind, and it is not the most important. But it is a good way to develop your thinking skills. That is one important reason to learn physics.

The other reason I think it is important to learn physics, which is going to sound really strange at first, but I hope will make more sense by the end of the year, is beauty. Physics is beautiful, and you were made for beauty. It takes time and hard work to see it, but it is worth it. This is true for most subjects. There is beauty there, but it takes work to be able to experience that beauty. I will come back to this at the end of the year and give a whole lecture on physics and beauty.

So why go to school and why learn physics? To reach your full intellectual potential and to experience beauty. I realize that might not make a lot of sense now, but I hope it does in the future. I look forward to learning along with all of you this year.

# 3. Have You Ever Seen the Number 2?

Have you ever seen the number two?

*Stunned silence. Again, they think I'm crazy.*

What do you think? What does the number 2 look like? And, by the way, I am not talking about poop.

*Laughter*

I am talking about the number itself. Do you see it anywhere in the room? Can you point to it?

"It's right there on the clock."

Is that the number two?

*More silent, wide-eyed stares, but a couple of students hesitantly indicate affirmation.* "Yes(?)"

What about this?

*I write "2" on the board.*

Is that the number 2?

*Some shy nods.*

Well, I have news for you. This is not the number two.

*Shock and dismay.*

This is a symbol that represents the number two. The fact is that you have never seen the number two.

Here is another example.

*I write the word "dog" on the board.*

Is that a dog?

"No."

*Students shake their heads.*

Right. That is not a dog. That is a word that represents the idea of dog that lives inside of your head or a particular dog that you might know or experience. A dog is a physical thing that lives in the world outside of you, and the word is a pointer to that thing or the idea of it in your mind. The word even comes in different forms. It can be the written word, or it can be a sound. When I say "dog" I am creating vibrations in the air that your ear receives and your brain interprets, but those sound waves themselves are not "dog," but a symbol that points to dog.

It is the same with this symbol that represents the number two. There are other symbols.

*I write "II," "two," and the Hebrew letter Bet on the board.*

We usually use the Arabic symbol, but this is the Roman symbol, the word itself spelled out, and the Hebrew Symbol for the number two. The difference between the number two and a dog, though, is that the number two is not a physical thing. Even if I hold two markers, these are two markers, not the number two. Like all mathematical things, you know what it is, and you can think about it and do all kinds of things with it, but you cannot see or touch it because it only exists in a mind.

"Everything I have learned is a lie."

*Laughter.*

Not quite. You are just now at a point where you can start to learn in a deeper way about the things you already know. This is what philosophy is about, starting to really question the things you think you know, seeing if you really know them, and asking what is really true.

But let me caution you. A few years ago a student left this class after learning about the number two, and he told his math teacher that the number two does not exist and so her job does not exist. Please don't do that. There is also a way of abusing philosophy by using it as a stick just to beat ideas you don't like or to put people down. The lifeblood of true philosophy is wonder and a desire for wisdom.

So, happy Philosophy Friday. I can't guarantee that it will always be this mind-blowing, but I hope it makes you think a little deeper about things.

# 4. How Do You Know the Earth Goes around the Sun?

Today I am going to start with a very simple question: how do *you* know that the earth goes around the sun?

"The clouds moving in the sky."

Well, couldn't that just be explained by wind and movement of the air in the atmosphere?

"True."

"What about how the sun is higher in the summer and lower in the sky in the winter?"

Good point. But, isn't that just the sun moving and being in different positions? Why does that mean that the earth is moving?

"Oh yeah. Ok."

*Silence*

So, *do* you believe that the earth goes around the sun?

*Heads nod.*

Ok, why?

"I guess because our teachers taught us."

That right! So, do you have any evidence for yourself that the earth goes around the sun?

*Heads shake.*

So, you all believe that the earth goes around the sun because that is what you have been taught, and you trust your teachers. For 99.9% of the people on this planet, the earth's movement is a matter of faith. Anthony Rizzi, a theoretical physicist, has pointed this out. I am sure that you all thought you knew for sure that the earth goes around the sun, but when we think about, it we realize that we really don't know for ourselves. If you want to know for yourself, you have to make some precise telescopic observations over a period of at least 6 months and work through the physics of gravitation discovered by Isaac Newton. Without those things, you have no evidence for yourself that the earth goes around the sun.

First of all, keep this in mind whenever you hear about groups of people and cultures from the past who thought the earth did not move. Up until the 1700's, that was what all the good science pointed to. There simply was no evidence that the earth moved. Even Galileo couldn't prove that the earth goes around the sun, though he thought he could. We tend to think that people were idiots because they thought the earth didn't move. People weren't so stupid after all prior to the modern period.

Second, philosophy is sometimes the process of having to unlearn things that we think we know. You thought you knew the earth goes around the sun. Well, it turns out that you don't really know that for yourself. You only believe that because that is what all your teachers have taught you. It is not easy to realize we don't know something as certainly as we thought or that we were wrong about something, and it is especially difficult when it comes to changing our minds about fundamental beliefs. It takes time to learn how to question the things we never ask questions about. Examine everything, even your assumptions. Some assumptions may turn out to be necessary, but you may find that some of your assumptions are not reliable. Philosophy is about pursuing truth at all costs.

Third, this brings up the distinction made by philosophers between two types of knowledge: knowledge and opinion. Knowledge is something that we know very well because we know why we know it. Most of the time, these are ideas that we know from experience. Opinion is a weaker form of knowledge; and opinion is an idea that we think is true, but we don't have a lot of evidence for it, or we place our trust in what someone else has said. Your knowledge about the moving earth is not really knowledge, but opinion. That doesn't mean it's not true or false.

Opinions are still true or false, they either match with reality or not. Every statement, once it is clearly understood, is either true or false, but whether it is knowledge or opinion has to do with *how* you know it or *why* you believe it.

Unfortunately, students are sometimes taught to distinguish between fact and opinion, but that is a false dichotomy. How many of you have been taught fact versus opinion? You are given statements and have to say if it is a fact or an opinion?

*Most if not all hands go up.*

Right. Listen. Every statement is either true or false. Tell me some statement that is usually taught to you as an opinion statement.

"Chocolate is the best flavor of ice cream."

Ok. The question is, what is the content of that statement? If I say that chocolate is the best, I might mean simply that chocolate is my favorite flavor of ice cream. And in that case, I am either telling the truth or I am not. I am either telling the truth about my favorite flavor of ice cream, or I am lying about my favorite flavor of ice cream. Or maybe I mean that the majority of people like chocolate ice cream. In that case, maybe I have conducted a survey or a poll of some kind. One way or another, once we have figured out the content of the statement, it is either true or false, fact or fiction.

Believe it or not, that kind of fact or opinion thinking is a form of brainwashing. The statement, "That's just your opinion," is a thought stopper. It actually arrests thinking instead of pushing you to think critically. One psychologist called it a thought-arresting cliché. Again, every statement either matches with reality, or it does not, once you figure out the meaning. If the content is not clear, that doesn't make it not true or false, it just means it needs to be investigated or clarified.

So, Happy Philosophy Friday!

# 5. What is Logically Wrong with This Statement?

*As students walk in, this is written on the board:*

*What is logically wrong with the following statement:*

*"Science is the only way to know what is true."*

Good morning everyone. Our Philosophy Friday question is on the board. This statement expresses an idea that is very common in society today, that science is the only real standard of knowledge. Everything else is just opinion. It is very subtle, and most people don't even realize they have this idea. But, there is something logically wrong with it. It's actually irrational. What do you think?

"Well, that's not true because there are other ways of knowing things."

Like what?

"We know things about history. That's not science."

But what if someone said that's not really knowledge because it's not scientific?

"I would disagree."

Ok. But you still haven't shown the logical problem with the statement itself.

*Silence.*

Let's think about science for a minute. How does it work? What have we been working on here in class?

"Experiments."

"Hypotheses."

Right. Making experiments to test hypotheses. Science deals with questions about patterns in the physical world that we can test. But what about this statement?

*I point to the statement "Science is the only way to know what is true."*

Is this a scientific statement? Is this a statement about physical patterns in the world that can be tested?

"No."

"Yes."

What experiment could you do to test this idea?

"You could try to find out what is true and see if it is science."

That's a little vague. How would you tell if a statement is true? The statement assumes at the beginning what the standard of truth is.

"So, there is no experiment."

Right. This statement is not a statement that can be tested. This is not a scientific statement. Instead, this is a philosophical statement about science. Think about it this way. If I draw a bunch of circles on the board representing the different fields of knowledge and labeled them...

*I draw a number of circles on the board and label them "Math," "Philosophy," "Science," "History."*

...where would this statement go?

"Philosophy."

Right.

*I draw an "x" in the philosophy circle.*

But, here is the problem. This statement is saying that the science circle is the only one that counts. It crosses off all the other circles, including...

*I cross of all the other circles.*

...the philosophy circle where this statement is. According to the statement, we cannot know if the statement is true. This is what we call a self-refuting statement. It crosses itself out. It cannot be true. This is a logical problem with the statement itself. It crosses off its own category. It cuts off its own legs. This is like sitting on a branch and sawing off the branch you are sitting on. The branch is philosophy, and the saw is the statement.

Again, I realize that this is a very popular idea today, but, as you can see, it makes no sense. It is illogical for someone to claim that they know it is true.

This is the process of philosophy. Learning to look critically at ideas that may be very popular and see if they really make sense. We all end up with all kinds of crazy ideas, so we need to clean house. But it is tough to give up old ideas. I once had a colleague who made this statement in a conversation. We were talking about stuff, I forget what, and he said almost this exact thing, that science is the only real way to know. I explained to him, just as I did to you, that the statement is self-refuting. He saw and understood what I meant, but then he said, "Well, I am just not saying it right." I am still waiting for him to tell me the right way to say it. Humility and the ability to admit that we are wrong is so important for philosophy!

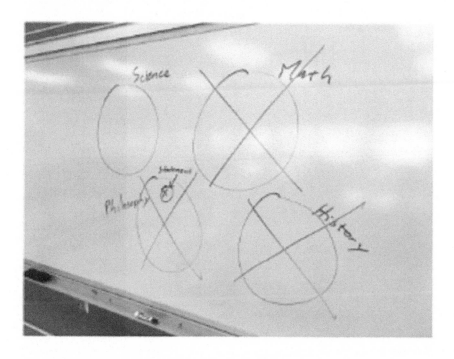

# 6. What is Logically Wrong with This Statement? (2)

*As students walk in, this is written on the board:*

*What is logically wrong with the following statement:*

*"There is no truth."*

Good morning everyone. Our philosophy Friday question is on the board. Like last week, there is a logical problem with this statement. And, like last week, this statement expresses a very common opinion in society today, the idea that there is no truth, that truth is relative, that we make our own reality.

"What is truth?"

Great, great question! Thank you for asking. That is a fundamental question. And the answer is actually pretty simple. Truth is just the correspondence between a statement and reality. If I make a statement that the board is white, and that statement actually matches the reality of the board, then it is true. If I say that the board is green, and that doesn't match with the reality of the board, then it is false. Aristotle defined truth in a way that only uses single-syllable words when translated into English, and I have it on the wall.

*I point to one of the quotes on my wall. See the appendix.*

To say of what is, that it is, and of what is not, that it is not, is true.

*As I say that, I can see students trying to follow.*

"What?"

So, if I say of something that it is, and it actually is, then it is true. If I say of the board that it is white, and it *is* white, then that is true. It just has to do with whether the statement or idea matches with the reality it's talking about.

Back to the statement, then, what is wrong with it logically?

"It's wrong because we can make true statements, like the board is white and it is sunny today."

Ok. I agree. We can give examples of true statements. But there is actually a logical problem with the statement itself, like last week. Think back to last week's statement.

"Is it that if there is no truth, then this statement isn't true?"

Right! That's it.

"What? I don't get it."

Look. If there is no truth, that means there are no true statements, including this one. That means, even this statement is not true.

"Oh."

*The light bulbs are turning on.*

So, it's self-refuting, just like last week's. It cannot be true. Here is another example.

*I write on the board "This statement is false."*

Is this statement true or false?

"It's false."

Well, if it is false, then it is false that it is false, and that means it is true.

*Confused looks.*

But if it is true, then it is true that it is false, and it is false.

"Ummm...you lost me."

Look at what it is saying. It is saying that it is false. If it is true, then it is false.

"So, this is self-refuting, too?"

Yes, in a way, because it turns out that this statement doesn't even really have any content. The first statement was making a claim and actually has some content. It refers to something. It has a meaning. This statement that "this statement is false" is just nonsense. You may as well be saying, "Blah, blah, blah."

*Laughter.*

But I hope you are seeing this powerful tool of logic. There are a lot of ideas floating around today, some of them you might even believe and not realize you believe, that don't really make sense when you think about them logically. The ideas that there is no truth and that science is the only way to know are very common, but ultimately irrational.

# 7. Any Superpower?

If you could have any superpower, what would it be and why?

"Shape-shifting."

Ok, why?

"So, I can turn into a cockroach or something and crawl under a locked door."

Why are you wanting to get into locked doors?

"So, if I wanted to rob a bank or something like that."

Anybody else?

"Mind control!"

Mind control? Why?

"So I could make people do what I want."

"Be invisible."

Why do you want to be invisible?

"So I can be a spy."

Why do you want to be a spy?

"So that I can get information."

Why do you want to get information?

"I don't know. So I can have power, because information is power."

Ah, I see, so you can have power. Ok, so here is the point. Let' see why this is a philosophical question. First of all, it is a psychological question. You give the reason for your superpower, and that reveals what you think is going to make you really happy. Money, power, control...whatever it might be. But this is very common. I think most people think that these things will make them really happy.

The question in philosophy is what is the ultimate good? What is real happiness? And not just happiness in the feeling

23

sense; we are asking about the *summum bonum*, the greatest good. This is the fundamental question in a whole category in philosophy: ethics. It is about the best way to live your life, and the idea is that the greatest good is going to bring us the greatest happiness.

So, the superpower question is to tease out what you think is going to really make you happy, and the job of philosophy is to investigate if that really will make you happy.

Regarding what you said before, that information is power, there is a famous quote that says almost the same thing, "Knowledge is power," but there is another quote that power tends to corrupt. So, is it good to have a lot of power? Can a person who is corrupt have that deep joy and happiness that we are all after, whether we realize it or not?

How often have we thought about the way we live our lives and intentionally asked ourselves, "Is what I am doing right now going to lead me to real happiness?" Or how many times have we even consciously thought about what real happiness is? This is one of the big questions in philosophy, and it stands at the foundation of everything we do. It seems like an "out there" kind of idea, but it is actually very practical.

# 8. What is Respect?

Good morning everyone. This is "Respect Week", and teachers have been asked to talk about respect or do some kind of activity. This is perfect for Philosophy Friday, because this is within the realm of philosophy. Discussions about what respect is and whether we should respect each other are part of ethics, and ethics is one of the big categories in philosophy.

So, we will discuss two things. What is respect? It is important to know what we are talking about, so we should define our terms. And, why should we or should we not respect one another?

"Respecting means accepting everyone. Not treating them any differently."

So, what do you mean by 'not treating them any differently?' Is that the same thing as accepting?

"It's part of accepting."

"Respect is treating people how you want to be treated. So you wouldn't do something that you wouldn't want them to do."

"I think it's treating people a little better than you want to. It's like you understand or admire them or something they do. You recognize that they can do something harder or they have some quality you yourself don't have."

"Respect is when you treat someone kindly and think about their feelings."

"Everybody has something unique, and we should respect that. Everyone is good at something."

What if my unique thing is robbing banks?

*Laughter*

"Uh...ok."

*Silence*

Should you respect everyone, or should people have to earn your respect?

"I think people should have to *keep* your respect. Respect everyone to start with, but then don't if they lose your respect. Like if robbing banks is your thing, then you would lose my respect."

So, we *should* respect other people?

*Nodding heads.*

"Yes."

And *should* we lose respect for people if they do something mean? Or if they subtweet you, or something?

*Laughter.*

"I think you should lose respect for them, but you shouldn't treat them badly, like you should still respect them but not have respect for them."

"She lost me."

"I see what she means."

What we are seeing here is that there are different definitions of this word. Let's say you start a new job, and there is someone who doesn't give you the time of day and is maybe even rude to you. They are supposed to get something to you, and they get it to you late and don't even apologize for it. They have even made some rude comments about your work. Do you respect that person or not? Has that person lost your respect?

"No, I don't think you have to respect them."

"Well, don't treat them badly because you wouldn't want them to treat you that way."

Let's take the next step now and say that you find out that person recently lost a child and just came back the day before you arrived at work. Does that change the way you respect that person?

"Yeah."

And how often do we really know what is going on in someone's life? Let's face it, we are all broken inside, we all have issues, we all have stuff going on. And the worst issue is to think that you don't have any issues.

But let's take this to a different level. The "why" part. We should or shouldn't respect people. Why? Let's say that I'm an anarchist. I don't care about your respect. If you disrespect me, I don't care. I think that's what we should do. Survival of the fittest. Every man for himself. Why should I respect you? That's my belief system. Why are you going to impose your morals on me?

"Well, it's just human decency."

I don't care about human decency; I don't believe in it. I think it's just a construct that weak people have built into society because they don't want to be hurt. So, the question is, do we think that people *ought* to respect each other? If so, *Why?* Or is that just what you want people to do?

"If it's at work or school where we are working towards a common goal, we have to."

Right! And realize that is a qualified 'have to.' We respect one another *if we want to* get this thing to happen. But is there an unqualified *ought*? Without appealing to getting a job done or wanting society to function a certain way? Or do we want other people to respect each other simply because that's what we want, and we are telling other people how to live their lives?

*Silence.*

Not an easy question to answer. *But!* There are answers to questions like this in philosophy, and this is actually a big topic in philosophy. What is the best way to live your life? What is the good way to live? This is ethics. And people have written about this for centuries. One of the problems as we discuss this is that all of us in this room are products of our society, and it might be that our society has missed something important. We are so quick to look at other societies, especially ancient societies and say, 'They were so stupid because they did this and this.' What are the things we do and believe that people 200 years from now are going to look at and say, 'We can't believe they thought that!' That's not to say that our society is right or their society will be right, but just that we should be careful. That is one of the reasons we need to read great books from other time periods, so that we can see around some of our own blind spots. But there are answers, and there are good arguments on different sides of the 'why.'

Sometimes, Philosophy Friday is going to be a little disappointing because I am not going to just say, 'Ok, here's the answer.' But I don't want you to walk away thinking there is no answer.

# 9. The Ring of Gyges

For Philosophy Friday we are going to do a follow up to last week's question, "What is respect?" If you remember, we did not come to a conclusion by the end. I was playing devil's advocate and asking what is respect in the first place. And also, why be respectful at all? Who cares? And then the week before that I asked if you could have any superpower, what would it be and why? In general, most people choose things that are 1) for their own pleasure or enjoyment, or 2) superpowers that they can use to take advantage of other people and get their own way. Rob banks, mind reading, money, pleasure, power, whatever. And how you answered that question was an indicator to you of what you think will make you really happy. In philosophy, we want to ask these questions. What is it that constitutes the best life? What is the good life? And then, like we were discussing last week, are there good reasons for being a respectful person? And what does respect mean in the first place?

The last two weeks relate to this story, which comes from a book written 2400 years ago called *The Republic*. In some English classes you read the allegory of the cave, and that is also from *The Republic*. The book is written by Plato, but it portrays Socrates going to Piraeus, and then he is on his way home to Athens, and someone stops him and invites him to his home. So they go to the home of Cephalus, an old man, and they sit down and begin talking. Cephalus, when asked, says that one of the advantages of being rich is that having money allows him to be a just man because he is able to pay back his debts. Socrates then asks Cephalus, "What is justice? Is it only paying back your debts and telling the truth?" Cephalus says, "Yes." Socrates then asks what he should do if someone lent him his sword but then went insane and wanted his sword back. Is it just to give the sword back to him? Cephalus says that he would not give the sword back. Socrates points out that justice, then, is not just telling the truth and paying debts, because in the case of his friend, giving back the sword would be telling the truth and paying back a debt. Cephalus realizes that he gave an inadequate definition, but he leaves. Someone else takes up the discussion, and it turns into a knock-'em-down, drag-em-out argument. They are calling each other names, one of them calls Socrates a baby, he should clean up his drool. And the first book ends without any clear definition of justice.

So, the project for the rest of the book is to figure out what justice is. That word for justice is sometimes translated as righteousness. So, what does it mean to live justly, to live righteously? What does it look like to live a just life? And secondly, is it worth it? Is a just man a happy man? And this word for happiness in Ancient Greek is tough to translate. It might mean more like "living well," "thriving" as a human being. Will living a just life bring you that kind of happiness, or is it better to commit injustice? So, at the beginning of book 2, they are setting up these questions. This story is part of the set up. They want to make the case as hard as possible for Socrates, so that he can then try to find his way out of this. This story is called the Ring of Gyges. Read along with me. I am going to stop and comment on it as we go along.

> Now that those who practice justice do so involuntarily and because they have not the power to be unjust will best appear if we imagine something of this kind:

So, he is saying ultimately that people who are good are good only because they need to be. They are not good because they want to be, but because they can't be bad and get away with it. They are weak or stupid, but if they were stronger or more clever, everyone would commit injustice and get away with it.

...having given both to the just and the unjust power to do what they will, let us watch and see whither desire will lead them; then we shall discover in the very act the just and unjust man to be proceeding along the same road, following their interest, which all natures deem to be their good, and are only diverted into the path of justice by the force of law.

They are saying, if we gave the good and the bad alike power to do whatever they wanted, we will see that everyone goes down the path of doing what we would call bad things.

The liberty which we are supposing may be most completely given to them in the form of such a power as is said to have been possessed by Gyges the ancestor of Croesus the Lydian.

Croesus was a ruler of Lydia, and there was this legend about how his ancestor came to have power.

According to the tradition, Gyges was a shepherd in the service of the king of Lydia; there was a great storm, and an earthquake made an opening in the earth at the place where he was feeding his flock. Amazed at the sight, he descended into the opening, where, among other marvels, he beheld a hollow brazen horse, having doors, at which he stooping and looking in saw a dead body of stature, as appeared to him, more than human, and having nothing on but a gold ring; this he took from the finger of the dead and re-ascended.

So, there is a huge storm. The earth opens up, he goes down, finds a horse with a man inside it, sees a ring, and takes it. A story about finding a ring? Sound familiar? It's going to sound more familiar.

Now the shepherds met together, according to custom, that they might send their monthly report about the flocks to the king; into their assembly he came having the ring on his finger, and as he was sitting among them he chanced to turn the collet of the ring inside his hand, when instantly he became invisible to the rest of the company and they began to speak of him as if he were no longer present. He was astonished at this, and again touching the ring he turned the collet outwards and reappeared; he made several trials of the ring, and always with the same result-when he turned the collet inwards he became invisible, when outwards he reappeared.

J.R.R. Tolkien, the author of *The Lord of the Rings,* knew this story. He was very well educated in Ancient philosophy and mythology. I don't think that he would deny that this is where he got the idea for *The Lord of the Rings.* However, notice the compliment that Tolkien gave to the Hobbits. They just used it for games. They didn't use it for evil. Fascinating.

Whereupon he contrived to be chosen one of the messengers who were sent to the court; where as soon as he arrived, he seduced the queen, and with her help conspired against the king and slew him and took the kingdom.

Wow. That was fast. So, given the power to do what he wants and get away with it, he uses it for his own advantage to become king.

Suppose now that there were two such magic rings, and the just put on one of them and the unjust the other; no man can be imagined to be of such an iron nature that he would stand fast in justice. No man would keep his hands off what was not his own when he could safely take what he liked out of the market, or go into houses and lie with any one at his pleasure, or kill or release from prison whom he would, and in all respects be like a god among men. Then the actions of the just would be as the actions of the unjust; they would both come at last to the same point.

So, again, what he is saying is that, given the same power, everyone would commit injustice. They would all do whatever they want to seek their own advantage. If you were given unlimited power, and you could do whatever you want and get away with it so that no one would even know, what advantage would there be to being a good person?

> And this we may truly affirm to be a great proof that a man is just, not willingly or because he thinks that justice is any good to him individually, but of necessity, for wherever any one thinks that he can safely be unjust, there he is unjust.

They are setting up this challenge and arguing that people are only good because they have to be.

> For all men believe in their hearts that injustice is far more profitable to the individual than justice, and he who argues as I have been supposing, will say that they are right. If you could imagine any one obtaining this power of becoming invisible, and never doing any wrong or touching what was another's, he would be thought by the lookers-on to be a most wretched idiot, although they would praise him to one another's faces, and keep up appearances with one another from a fear that they too might suffer injustice.

So, they are saying that even if someone did get a magic ring and only did good things, people would praise him. They would say, "Oh, he's a nice man." But in their heart of hearts, if someone had that power and didn't abuse it, people would think he was an idiot. If you have that power, take advantage of it.

And whether you think this way or not, maybe we've all been brainwashed enough that we think, "Oh no! I wouldn't do that!" The question is why? What advantage is there? Is it more profitable to be just or unjust?

That's what the rest of the book is about. First of all, what is justice, and then is it more advantageous to be just or unjust in your actions? I'm not going to ruin the book for you and give you Plato's answer, but hopefully this will encourage you to think about this more deeply.

And! Realize that you can only get so far if you think about this by yourself. One of the things you should learn to do is to bring into conversation the great minds of the past. You can talk to Plato; you can talk to Aristotle; you can talk to Thomas Aquinas, these great philosophers, through their books. They are not here in their physical presence, but they are here in the thoughts they have left. And if you have never had a conversation with a book, then you've never really read a book. As you are going along, you should be asking the author questions or summarizing what he is saying. Even Isaac Newton said...I have the quote over here somewhere...

*I go over to one of my walls where I know this quote is.*

Here it is... "If I have seen further than others, it is because I have stood on the shoulders of giants." He was able to do what he did because there was a lot of other stuff in place that others had done. And even this quote, his idea, he stole that, too. Here is another quote from someone else, Bernard of Chartres, and he said, "We are like dwarves, seated on the shoulders of giants. We see more things than the Ancients, and things more distant, but it is due neither to the sharpness of our sight, or the greatness of our stature, it is simply because they have left us their own."

Any questions about any of this stuff?

"In order to talk with a book, you need to ask it questions?"

Yup.

"And do you get an answer?"

Yes! I have had that happen. Good writers will do that. I have had times where I am reading a book, and I read something that doesn't make sense or comes out of nowhere, and I say, "Time out." So, I write a question in the margin, and then that question is answered a couple of pages later. And that happens quite a bit with Plato because his writings are in the form of a dialogue.

One of the important things to do is to meet the author on his own terms. We tend to read things today and just judge as we go along instead of really entering into the world and mind of the author. We play psychologist. We tend to say things like,

"Well, the author only said this because he was the product of a Patriarchal society... These ideas are not very modern..." instead of looking objectively at the full picture he paints and then asking, "Is it true? Does this argument make sense? What is valuable here?" We should approach a book, especially an old book, first as a student rather than as a critic. Be critical, but only because you are trying to learn, not criticize and ridicule. There is a big difference.

# 10. Pick a Quote or Two

*I have over 120 quotes posted on the walls of my classroom, and I keep adding more as I continue to read. The current list of quotes is in the appendix.*

Take a few minutes, read as many quotes as you can, and then pick out one or two that you think are interesting, you have a question about, you agree with or disagree with.

*Students walk around the room and look at the quotes, as instructed.*

All right, guys. Take a seat. When I am reading, I put a star next to anything I find interesting and want to keep. So, I actually have hundreds of pages of quotes from books I've read. These are ones appropriate to physics, philosophy or teaching. So, what did you guys find? Anything?

"I like the one about how people are schooled but not educated. I think that's true because if you like the classes you are in, you show an effort and have an interest in it, then it benefits you more because you learn it better. If you just memorize and repeat it, you will forget about it because you don't really value it. It is a waste of your time."

What's the difference between being schooled and being educated?

"Being schooled is just going to school, just going through the motions. Being educated is actually wanting to be involved in the class and trying to retain the information that you're being taught."

It's an interesting question to think about. The word *educate* means, by the way, to lead out. The *e* part comes from the Latin prefix *ex-* meaning "out," like exit, and the *duc* part comes from the Latin word *ducere* which means "to lead." So, educate means to lead out. The question then is: out of what are we lead, and into what?

"To lead out of school."

*Laughter.*

And there is another corresponding quote, "Only the educated are free." It means that only those who have been "lead out" are free. Did you happen to catch who said that quote?

*No response. Students start looking for the quote.*

Thomas More. He's actually a saint in the Catholic Church, and there was a movie made about him: *A Man for All Seasons.* He was put to death because he opposed some decisions the king was making. In the quote he says, "One of the problems of our time..." and his time was the sixteenth century. It was a problem even then.

Other quotes?

"I like the one that says, 'Light travels faster than sound. That's why some people appear bright until they speak.'"

I picked that because it's funny and it relates to physics. The speed of light is much, much faster than the speed of sound.

"'Man by nature desires to know.' We are all curious, and being curious is the only way to expand our knowledge."

Did you catch who said that one?

"Aristotle."

Yeah, Aristotle, Greek guy. Actually, there is a connection between that quote and the "Gnothi Seauton" quote, the one written in Greek. Gnothi Seauton was inscribed above the door of the Delphic Oracle, and that played a role in inspiring Socrates to become a philosopher. It means to know oneself; it's about knowing. Socrates was the teacher of Plato, and Plato was the teacher of Aristotle. "Man by nature desires to know." Those are the first words of one of his books.

That quote implies that, since it is part of our nature to know, then in learning, in knowing, in being "educated" in this broader sense, we fulfill our nature and reach our full potential as human beings. On the flip side, if we ever lose our curiosity and stop asking the big questions, then we have become something less than human. That's what he's implying.

"'Some drink at the fountain of knowledge; others just gargle.'"

Yeah. I thought that was funny. Some of you were talking about this quote over here: "Just as the suitors of Penelope consorted with her maidservants when they were not able to approach the Queen herself..." Do you guys know this story about Odysseus? Odysseus was away, Penelope was his wife. All these suitors came to gain her attention, but they consorted with her servants because they could not get to Penelope. Just as that happened, "So also do those who are not able to approach true wisdom wear themselves thin over the other kinds of education which have no value." [Bion] So, when it comes to the fountain of knowledge, schooling versus education, there are some kinds of knowledge that are better than others, some that are more applicable, some that we want to know at a deeper level. Wisdom versus just information.

"'Herein is the evil of ignorance, that he who is neither good nor wise is nevertheless satisfied with himself.'"

And that was Socrates or Plato who said that. Socrates didn't write anything down. It's Plato writing, but he puts it in the mouth of Socrates. I have that same quote up somewhere else, just a different translation, and it says that the really damaging thing about stupidity is its self-satisfaction. People who are foolish don't know that they are foolish. That's a bit of a problem.

"'Aesthetic criteria are enormously valuable in forming our judgments.'"

Yeah. Do you know what aesthetic means? It means having to do with beauty. At the beginning of the year I told you that beauty was one of the important reasons to learn physics. Not only do we by nature desire to know, but we also by nature desire beauty, beauty in its deeper sense. The person who said that was Roger Penrose, a theoretical physicist and one of Stephen Hawking's Ph.D. thesis advisors. He is saying that beauty plays an important role in the decisions that theoretical physicists make. We usually think of physics and science as cold, mathematical, calculative, unbiased, rational, just experiment driven, but that is not the case. Theoretical physicists will all say that beauty plays a big role in their judgments as scientists. That's pretty fascinating.

"'Wherever the truth of our judgments, opinions, or beliefs is a proper concern, we should be prepared to argue with those who disagree with us, with the firm hope that our disagreement can be resolved'" [Mortimer Adler].

So, be open to argument. Plato said that one of the worst things that can happen to a person is that he learns to hate arguments. That doesn't mean that you get angry with each other, but you are willing to discuss. Nowadays ... I don't know, maybe it's always been the case ... the tendency is to just not even talk with someone we disagree with. I've had discussions with people where people start yelling or crying because things get so personal. But it's those things that we really want to find out about. But, the other part of this is that you should be able to defend your beliefs, the things you think are true, because if you can't defend them, then you don't really know them. Remember, we talked about how you think the earth goes around the sun. How do you know that? Because you've listened to other people. And what about things more fundamental than that, because it doesn't make much a difference to the way you live your life if the earth goes around the sun or not. There are a lot of other questions that do make a difference. Make sure you spend time thinking about the big questions and talking about them and reading about them.

# 11. Two Weeks Left to Live

Imagine you are told that in two weeks you are going to die. There is no disease; you can't cure it; you won't feel any pain; it will be instantaneous. You are just going to drop dead in two weeks. It's not that the whole world is ending. It's just you. How do you spend your time?

*I can tell they are still thinking about how they can get out of this one.*

"Spend my money."

Spend the money! Ok, spend on what?

"Travel places."

"Sky-diving."

"Is it only you who is going to die?"

Yes. Only you. No one is going to kill you. You are just going to die.

"I am going to spend my money to find a way to stop it."

There's no getting out of it.

*Someone says something, but I can't hear it, and everyone else laughs.*

What did you say?

"I said finish the AP Physics packet."

*I give my AP Physics class a whole unit as a single packet of notes and problems. When they finish the packet, they are ready for that unit's test.*

*Laughter, again.*

Finish the packet. There you go. But would you bother? Would you even come to school?

"NO! no."

"I would watch movies straight for two weeks."

That's a lot of movies.

"Eat anything I want."

"I would try to make a legacy in the last two weeks."

What kind of a legacy? Because we can leave all kinds of legacies, right?

"A memorable, good one."

A memorable, good one. Fair enough. There are a lot of ways of making it memorable. But, what makes a legacy a good one?

"You have to do something nice."

That's it?

"I don't know."

*Laughter.*

"I would buy life insurance."

*Laughter.*

I think that would involve you in fraud, because I think you would need to disclose something important on the form, like the fact that you are going to die.

"But you don't know why."

"You could frame someone for your murder."

*Laughter.*

There you go. That's a legacy. Deceit.

"Bike from here to Niagara Falls."

In philosophy we face a lot of these "man on a desert island" type of situations. And they are useful, but we have to remember that they only go so far. The fact is that if you were really faced with the reality that you were going to die in two weeks, it would most likely rearrange all of your priorities in life. It's hard to place yourself in that situation. But we can imagine as best we can and then ask what really would be the best way to spend your time in your last two weeks.

And that brings us to the question about what is the good life? What is the best way to live your life? What is it that I really value? The answer we give is what we *think* is going to make us happy, or what we think will make other people happy. The next question is this: are those things really going to make us happy, give us true happiness?

Now, I am not giving you the news that you are dying in two weeks in reality. But, you *are* going to die. You do have a limited amount of time. I can tell you that in my time as a teacher, I have had two former students die.

"What?"

Yeah. It was within a year or two of when they graduated. One contracted a disease that they couldn't get a hold of, and the other had a massive stroke. It's a reality. You don't know when you are going to die, and you can't control it.

But I say that to drive home this idea that it is well worth the time to think about what the best way to live your life is. Whether it is two weeks or two decades, it's still finite. Don't you want to be intentional about how you live it? Socrates said, "The unexamined life is not worth living." And that is not encouragement to commit suicide if your life is unexamined, but it is an admonition to examine your life and the meaning of your existence. What is the good life?

That is a fundamental question in philosophy. What is the good life? And most philosophers don't say things like money and houses and comfort. They give really interesting answers and some good arguments behind those answers. Worth looking into.

And that's all I've got for this week.

# 12. Painful Truth or Comforting Illusion

True or false? It is better to believe a painful truth than a comforting illusion.

"Wait. Could you repeat that?"

It's on the board.

"Oh!"

"Do you know what the truth is?"

Yes. Let's say for now that you believe something, but you know it's an illusion, and you choose to believe it anyway.

"I think it's true because, even though it might feel better to believe a comforting illusion, knowing the truth is what makes you a stronger person. Facing your reality. I don't think you should live your life lying to yourself to make yourself feel better."

"I've done that. I have known the truth but denied it, and then it came back to me."

So, it would have been better to believe the painful truth in the first place?

"Yeah."

"I think you should expect the worst because you never know what is going to happen. It's better to be prepared for it, even though it might never happen."

So, you're saying that a painful illusion is better than a painful truth, because you are living in the illusion that the worst will happen.

*Some hesitation.* "Yeah."

Ok.

"I think it's true because you have to make adjustments in your life and you won't be able to make those adjustments if you don't know the truth."

Why do you have to make adjustments?

"Because you have to go through life...I don't know...I pass."

*Laughter.*

Well, you made a statement that we have to make adjustments, why?

"To make adjustments, to make your life better. If you find out something horrible you need to change."

But isn't comfort better than pain?

"Yeah, but... It depends. Like Santa Clause. You know he's not real..."

"What?!"

*Laughter.*

We are going to look at the physics of Santa Clause when the time comes.

"Don't worry guys, he's real. But you feel like you have to know the truth."

"I think you need to know the truth because otherwise you could really mess up somebody's life if you don't know in some difficult situation."

"In order to grow as a person, you need to be exposed to the truth. You have to come to understand the world better. While illusions are good short-term, they don't mentally prepare you for life."

But little kids are so happy. Why would you want to grow up mentally? Adults are cynical, angry and stressed.

"That's true."

"I think it's true because I would rather live in my truth than in an illusion someone else created for me. And the truth keeps changing."

Ok. This brings up a good point. We've talked about this before, but it's worth reviewing. What is truth? This is an important question. It's the correspondence between thought and reality. If the thought or the statement actually matches with the way things really are, then it' really true. So, there really isn't a "my truth" or "your truth" because there's only one reality, and truth has to do with that one reality. For example, I say that this board is white. If that statement matches with the reality of how the board really is, then it is true.

"But what if, because of the lighting or something, the board looks red."

Good question. What we do at that point is investigate further. We change the lighting. We bring in other people to see if they see the same thing we do. We double check. Sometimes appearances can be deceiving, but that just means we need to do some extra work to make sure we aren't deceived.

But that is a good point, too, because the light that we shine on reality is our own perceptions. We all see the world in a particular way, through our particular lenses and how we've been trained to look at the world. But we don't get to make reality. We don't get to make it up. We have to conform our lenses to reality, not make reality conform to our lenses. And the way we see things depends on the kind of person we are, the eyes that we've developed for ourselves.

"I think illusions are ways to avoid painful truths. So, with the little kids thing, I think little kids are so happy because they see the painful truth and they just say it. Little kids don't think about it; they just say things."

This is what philosophy is all about. The word *philosophy* means "the love of wisdom." And what is wisdom but the truth, whatever that truth might be? Philosophy is about this process of seeking truth, no matter the cost.

A lot of the things you guys are talking about are situational truths. For example, a kid finding out at 25 that he was adopted. In philosophy we want to know more fundamental truths like what the nature of reality is.

Another way of looking at this quote and figuring out what is best is to ask what your mind was made for? The mind was made for truth, and if you feed it anything else it will get sick and go bad. What is the function of the thing? What are we talking about here? The mind. What is the function of the mind? To know. We, by nature, want to know things.

The wording of the original question is also a little misleading because, since the mind was made for truth, any truth is good for it. The question associates pain with truth and comfort with illusion unnecessarily. Sometimes you have to question the question. The meaning of life is not comfort. I hate to tell you that. Comfort, pleasure, and entertainment are not what life is all about. Or maybe it is. Maybe one day one of you will prove me wrong.

# 13. What Makes the Good Guys the Good Guys and the Bad Guys the Bad Guys?

The question today is what makes the good guys the good guys and the bad guys the bad guys?

"There's no such thing as good guys."

No such thing as good guys. Why?

"Everyone has flaws. Everyone chooses to do things based on what he thinks."

So, no good, no bad?

"Yeah."

"I think that intentions make people good versus bad. Someone could do something bad but have good intentions. Like trying to give someone medicine to help them but accidentally giving too much and you kill them. That doesn't make you a bad person."

Ok. Right. Maybe the labeling was wrong on the medicine and you didn't know. Sure. You are just trying to help. Like Adolf Hitler. He had a vision of the next stage of human evolution, what society could be. He was just doing everything in the name of progress. So, what he did wasn't wrong either, right?

*A moment of stunned silence.*

"In *his* mind."

"It's all about perspective!"

Is it?

"Because in his mind he was doing the right thing."

Why were you all shocked when I said that it wasn't right or wrong? That's what he believed, so it really wasn't right or wrong?

"In our perspective what he did was wrong. He committed genocide."

"That's what he believed in."

That *is* what he believed in.

"Everyone believes in their own thing.

Ok. So let me ask you, is the conclusion then that what he did was not wrong?

*Silence.*

Killing millions of innocent people?

"He was a sicko."

So, you're saying that what he did was wrong.

"Yes."

"No."

Is it a matter of perspective, or is there really some standard that we can judge by?

"No, there's no standard."

So then he wasn't really a sicko.

"No, it's just from our perspective he was. Our opinion of the guy."

Ok. So, if we call him a sicko, it's only because *we* think what he did was wrong.

"Right, but in his mind, he thinks other people are sickos. But from our perspective we think that guy really needs some help."

But why does he need help if it's all just a matter of perspective?

*Silence.*

If it's all just a matter of perspective, then there is no right or wrong, no one needs help. It's just whatever each person wants. It's not *really* wrong to murder millions of innocent people. If we are going to label some things as bad or some things as good, why? Or, do we just label actions "bad" that we don't like?

Let's take a specific example, like murdering a toddler.

"That is dark. You don't have to go there!"

Well, this has happened in history. Child sacrifices. Taking a baby and putting it into an oven.

"I think that is sick."

Well, maybe that's just your perspective.

"I think the majority of society would say that's not right."

Is it majority rules?

"Pretty much."

But if you're in that society, the majority of people thought it was ok and actually beneficial. If you are in a society that thinks slavery is ok, does that make it ok?

"Well, that was their way of life."

True, but does that make it not wrong? Does that make it ok to treat some humans like non-humans?

"No, it's still wrong."

Ok, so it's not just a matter of majority rules.

"Yeah."

Ok. Why?

"I don't know. You wouldn't want to be treated like that."

So? Survival of the fittest.

"I don't know how to keep answering. You keep coming back with these questions so quick."

What I'm trying to get you to realize is a couple of things. If we have a set of beliefs, we want those beliefs to be consistent, to logically make sense. If we say something like, "Hitler was a sicko," and then say, "All of morality is just a matter of perspective," those two things don't line up with each other. They clash logically. Same with saying that majority rules. If you say that morality is just dictated by what everyone thinks, that also doesn't work with saying something like, "treating slaves as non-humans is wrong." So, what is the standard? Why is it wrong?

Now, hear me say this: I am not condoning treating people like slaves and I am not promoting genocide. I am just playing devil's advocate to get you to think about this a bit deeper. I am trying to push you a little bit.

So, what's the standard?

"Hitler had a chemical imbalance."

Well, what if his chemical balance was the right one and the rest of us have the wrong balance? What's the standard, and why does that make his actions wrong?

"Because people were just minding their own business. They didn't do anything to him."

So? Why does that mean he shouldn't hurt them?

"Well, in his mind he should, but he shouldn't."

But why? If you think he shouldn't, how would you convince him that he shouldn't.

"Because that would make the world a better place."

That's what he thought he was trying to do. Progress. Anything in the name of progress. We hear people talk about progress all the time. He *was* trying, from his perspective, to make the world a better place.

I also want to make clear that I am *not* saying that there is no standard. Most philosophers in history say that there is a standard. They just disagree about what the standard is. It was generally agreed upon until the 1600s. Now there are a few different philosophical theories about what makes right and wrong. But this is an important question, and it's in the realm of philosophy. Specifically, it's ethics.

If you major in business or something involved with medicine, it is likely that you'll have to take an ethics class. Business ethics. Medical ethics.

But I'm not going to give you the answer to this question.

"Why?"

Because I want you to think about it.

"But I don't think we're going to be able to come up with this answer on our own."

And that's just it. You don't have to reinvent the wheel. There are people who have discussed this for 2,500 years. There have been many books written about this. I make YouTube videos about some of these topics. Philosophy is a community enterprise. Get to know some of these philosophers and their ideas, but most importantly seek the truth.

# 14. Allegory of the Cave

Today we are going to read a classic story that comes from one of the most important works in Western History: the allegory of the cave from *The Republic*. I think some of you may have read this already. It is likely that you have already read references to this story, and it is very likely that you will encounter more references to this story as you read. Hopefully you read. *The Republic* is also where we got the story about the ring of Gyges, which we did a few weeks ago. So, same book, but much later in the book.

Plato uses this story as an allegory to illustrate his particular philosophy and method of education, but the story is applicable to philosophy in general. So, you guys can read one paragraph at a time, and as you read, I am going to do some drawing on the board and stop you along the way to explain things.

"Picture men dwelling in a sort of subterranean cavern with a long entrance open to the light on its entire width. Conceive them as having their legs and necks fettered from childhood, so that they remain in the same spot, able to look forward only, and prevented by the fetters from turning their heads. Picture further the light from a fire burning higher up and at a distance behind them, and between the fire and the prisoners and above them a road along which a low wall has been built, as the exhibitors of puppet-shows have partitions before the men themselves, above which they show the puppets."

"All that I see," he said.

"See also, then, men carrying past the wall implements of all kinds that rise above the wall, and human images and shapes of animals as well, wrought in stone and wood and every material, some of these bearers presumably speaking and others silent."

"A strange image you speak of," he said, "and strange prisoners."

"Like to us," I said;

Ok, stop. Pay attention to what he just said. This is a strange image, and these are strange prisoners. Then he says, "Like us." He is saying that, in some way, you and I are these prisoners. He's talking about *you* and *me*. Let's continue.

"For, to begin with, tell me do you think that these men would have seen anything of themselves or of one another except the shadows cast from the fire on the wall of the cave that fronted them?"

"How could they," he said, "if they were compelled to hold their heads unmoved through life?"

"And again, would not the same be true of the objects carried past them?"

"Surely."

"If then they were able to talk to one another, do you not think that they would suppose that in naming the things that they saw they were naming the passing objects?"

"Necessarily."

"And if their prison had an echo from the wall opposite them, when one of the passersby uttered a sound, do you think that they would suppose anything else than the passing shadow to be the speaker?"

"By Zeus, I do not," said he.

"Then in every way such prisoners would deem reality to be nothing else than the shadows of the artificial objects."

"Quite inevitably," he said.

Ok. So, as you can see, there are people bound hand, foot, and head. They can only look forward. All they ever see are shadows on the wall, and not even shadows of real things, but shadows of copies of things. And they hear echoes. But they think that is reality. They are looking at the shadow of a cutout of a dog.

*I refer to my sketch on the board.*

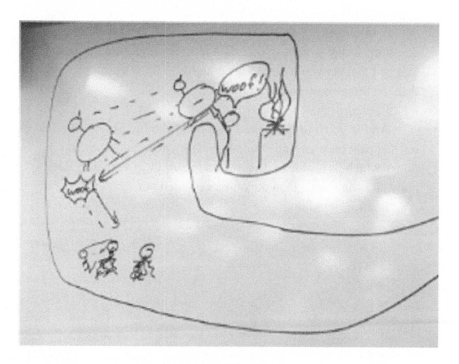

I know, I'm such a good artist, right?...

*Laughter.*

They are looking at the shadow of a cutout of a dog, and they think that's a real dog! They don't know the difference at all! But this is us. Plato is saying that, in some way, we don't see the things themselves, we only see some other kind of impression of things. We aren't seeing reality as it truly is, somehow.

"Consider, then, what would be the manner of the release and healing from these bonds and this folly if in the course of nature something of this sort should happen to them: When one was freed from his fetters and compelled to stand up suddenly and turn his head around and walk and to lift up his eyes to the light, and in doing all this felt pain and, because of the dazzle and glitter of the light, was unable to discern the objects whose shadows he formerly saw, what do you suppose would be his answer if someone told him that what he had seen before was all a cheat and an illusion, but that now, being nearer to reality and turned toward more real things, he saw more truly? And if also one should point out to him each of the passing objects and constrain him by questions to say what it is, do you not think that he would be at a loss and that he would regard what he formerly saw as more real than the things now pointed out to him?"

"Far more real," he said.

"And if he were compelled to look at the light itself, would not that pain his eyes, and would he not turn away and flee to those things which he is able to discern and regard them as in very deed more clear and exact than the objects pointed out?"

"It is so," he said.

Ok. Someone has come to set him free. Great! But he doesn't like it. He wants his old comfortable world. Everything else seems less real to him than the shadows, even though those other things are more real. But it hurts! It always hurts to realize that what we thought was true was only an illusion, like when you all realized at the beginning of the year that you don't really know for yourself that the earth goes around the sun and that you've never seen the number two.

Notice, too, that the prisoner doesn't do this himself. Someone has to come and set him free and force him to stand up and look around. We need people who will wake us up from our sleep of illusion. For Plato, that was Socrates.

"And if," said I, "someone should drag him thence by force up the ascent which is rough and steep, and not let him go before he had drawn him out into the light of the sun, do you not think that he would find it painful to be so haled along, and would chafe at it, and when he came out into the light, that his eyes would be filled with its beams so that he would not be able to see even one of the things that we call real?"

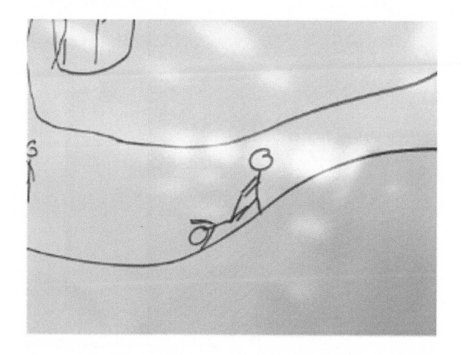

"Why, no, not immediately," he said.

This guy doesn't want to leave. He wants his old place. We like to hold on to our old ideas, and we get angry when some of our fundamental beliefs are challenged.

And have you ever had it happen that you are in some dark place and then you come out into the bright sunlight? And it hurts?

"Yeah."

It takes time for your eyes to adjust. Well, imagine someone who had *never* been out in daylight before. So, it really hurts!

"Then there would be need of habituation, I take it, to enable him to see the things higher up. And at first he would most easily discern the shadows and, after that, the likenesses or reflections in water of men and other things, and later, the things themselves, and from these he would go on to contemplate the appearances in the heavens and heaven itself, more easily by night, looking at the light of the stars and the moon, than by day the sun and the sun's light."

"Of course."

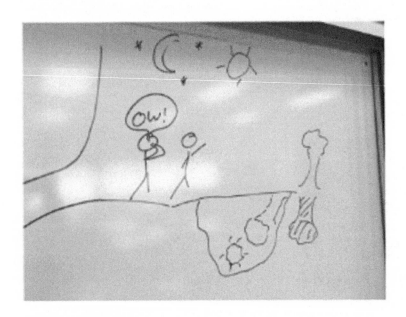

"And so, finally, I suppose, he would be able to look upon the sun itself and see its true nature, not by reflections in water or phantasms of it in an alien setting, but in and by itself in its own place."

"Necessarily," he said.

Ok. So, there is a process where he gets used to looking at things. First, he looks at things at nighttime, then at shadows and reflections of things, then things themselves. He started with shadows of copies of things, then moved on to copies of things, then shadows and reflections of the things themselves, and finally to things themselves. Now he can look at a real tree.

But even more than that, he can look at the sun, the source of all sight, and he can contemplate the sun in itself. For philosophers, this is the greatest good: to see and understand and contemplate the true nature of reality, the source of all being.

"And at this point he would infer and conclude that this it is that provides the seasons and the courses of the year and presides over all things in the visible region, and is in some sort the cause of all these things that they had seen."

"Obviously," he said, "that would be the next step."

"Well then, if he recalled to mind his first habitation and what passed for wisdom there, and his fellow-bondsmen, do you not think that he would count himself happy in the change and pity them?"

"He would indeed."

"And if there had been honors and commendations among them which they bestowed on one another and prizes for the man who is quickest to make out the shadows as they pass and best able to remember their customary precedences, sequences and co-existences, and so most successful in guessing at what was to come, do you think he would be very keen about such rewards, and that he would envy and emulate those who were honored by these prisoners and lorded it among them, or that he would feel with Homer and 'greatly prefer while living on earth to be serf of another, a landless man,' and endure anything rather than opine with them and live that life?"

"Yes," he said, "I think that he would choose to endure anything rather than such a life."

So, now he remembers the other people in the cave and what that life was like. He remembers that they used to play games where a shadow would show up on the wall and there would be a contest to see who could identify it first. And the winners would get prizes. Does he care about that anymore? Not at all. That whole world, while he loved it at the time, is like straw to him now, because now he knows about the real nature of things. He couldn't care less about all of those rewards. But! He remembers the people and he cares about them. He wants them to learn what he has learned. So, he goes back down to try to help them.

"And consider this also," said I, "if such a one should go down again and take his old place would he not get his eyes full of darkness, thus suddenly coming out of the sunlight?"

"He would indeed."

"Now if he should be required to contend with these perpetual prisoners in 'evaluating' these shadows while his vision was still dim and before his eyes were accustomed to the dark--and this time required for habituation would not be very short--would he not provoke laughter, and would it not be said of him that he had returned from his journey aloft with his eyes ruined and that it was not worthwhile even to attempt the ascent? And if it were possible to lay hands on and to kill the man who tried to release them and lead them up, would they not kill him?"

"They certainly would," he said.

So, he comes back down, and he can't compete with them because he is too used to seeing real things. They look at him and say, "You went out there, and now you're dumber! We're not going out there!" And they would kill him if they could. This, of course, is Socrates for Plato, because Socrates was put to death by the people of Athens. But isn't this what we tend to do to enlightened people? Jesus and Gandhi are other examples.

There's another similarity I want to draw here. What does this look like?

*I point to my drawing of the cave.*

A light coming from overhead and projecting an image on a large wall? People lined up in rows facing forward all the time?

"A classroom!"

*Our classrooms all have projectors hanging from the ceiling.*

Ok, yes! Good point! In some classrooms we put information up on the board and tell you what is what. But if you don't think about it for yourself or question it, it might be an illusion. Like that quote: many are schooled but few are educated. So, unfortunately, yes. I agree that school *can* be like that.

But there is another place I had in mind that is like this, where people actually pay money and go for entertainment.

"The movies!"

Right! The movies. And don't we think, when we are watching a movie, that *that* is real life? The drama, the vengeance, the beauty, the cars, the fame, the infatuation, the bling-bling, the money. That's what *real* life is, and our life is just some poor copy of that. But the movie life is the illusion, the shadow on the wall. Sometimes it can be a rude awakening to realize that we are missing out on the real life that is right in front of us and all around us all the time.

To add to the problem, we have now made the wall with the shadows really small and put them in our pockets. The world of social media, news headlines, slogans, soundbites, comment sections, propaganda and constantly streaming entertainment is not reality.

I have a few other passages that help to illustrate the point of this allegory. One of them is from *Anna Karenina* by Leo Tolstoy. I call this the anti-philosopher passage because it talks about the exact opposite of what a philosopher is striving for.

Stepan Arkadyevitch had not chosen his political opinions or his views; these political opinions and views had come to him of themselves, just as he did not choose the shapes of his hat and coat, but simply took those that were being worn.

This man doesn't hold his opinions because he has carefully though them through. Instead, he holds his opinions because they are fashionable.

And for him, living in a certain society – owing to the need, ordinarily developed at years of discretion, for some degree of mental activity – to have views was just as indispensable as to have a hat. If there was a reason for his preferring liberal to conservative views, which were held also by many of his circle, it arose not from his considering liberalism more rational, but from its being in closer accordance with his manner of life.

Instead of thinking about which view is the most rational, he chooses the opinions that best suit the way he wants to live. Tolstoy goes on to describe the views of the liberal party and how they suited Stepan. And then he continues.

And he liked his newspaper, as he did his cigar after dinner, for the slight fog it diffused in his brain…Having finished the paper, a second cup of coffee and a roll and butter, he got up, shaking the crumbs off the roll of his waistcoat; and, squaring his broad chest, he smiled joyously: not because there was anything particularly agreeable in his mind – the joyous smile was evoked by a good digestion.

He is controlled by his appetites, not his mind. This is a man who lives his life by the shadows on the wall, completely subject to the views of society.

I have a quote on my wall somewhere from one of my favorite writers, G.K. Chesterton, and it describes the prisoners in the cave and Stepan perfectly. "Millions of mild black-coated men call themselves sane and sensible merely because they always catch the fashionable insanity, because they are hurried into madness after madness by the maelstrom of the world." A maelstrom is a powerful whirlpool, by the way.

Here is a quote from a book on the history of philosophy by Frederick Copleston. "These prisoners represent the majority of mankind, that multitude of people who remain all their lives in a state of [the lowest and weakest kind of knowledge] beholding only shadows of reality and hearing only echoes of truth. Their view of the world is most inadequate, distorted by 'their own passions and prejudices, and the passions and prejudices of other people as conveyed to them by language and rhetoric.'" We live in an age where other peoples' passions and prejudices are communicated by language and rhetoric faster and in greater abundance than ever before. It is really hard to be aware of all that rhetoric, let alone sort through and evaluate all of it.

Anyway, that's beyond the time we have for today. Happy Philosophy Friday! Classic story, and it's all about the pursuit and love of truth.

# 15. What do you Know with Absolute Certainty?

For today, I want you to tell me what you know with absolute certainty. What is it that you know and that you cannot doubt?

"Who my parents are."

"I don't know about that."

"I hear a lot of baby mix ups happen."

"I could have a blood test."

True, but maybe they make a mistake at the lab. How do you know the information from the blood test is reliable?

"I know how I am feeling right now. I know about my feelings."

How do you know you are aware of your feelings? Maybe there are other feeling there you are not aware of? I know I used to think that my only feelings were hungry and tired. Turns out there are more. It's still a work in progress for me. Also, de-Nile [denial] is not just a river in Egypt.

*Confused looks.*

De-Ni-Al. Denial. Sounds like "the Nile," the river in Egypt.

"Oh!"

*They get it. Laughter.*

It is possible for people to deny how they are feeling, unfortunately. So, mostly, you know, but it is possible to doubt that you are well aware of your own emotions.

"I know that I'm breathing right now."

Have you guys ever seen *The Matrix*? It's a movie where robots and computers have taken over the world, and they are using humans as energy sources because we produce so much body heat. But the humans are in these little pods full of some liquid, and they are asleep. But, they have electrodes hooked up to their brains and nervous systems. The computers "pump" their experiences into them so that they think and feel like they are in the everyday world, just like what you are experiencing now, only their bodies are really curled up in that little cell. But they don't know the difference. So, maybe you are in the Matrix, and you're not *really* breathing right now.

"I know the laws of physics!"

*Laughter.*

How do you know all of this isn't just an illusion, and you just know the laws of your illusion?

"Well, I know they work in the illusion."

Ok. But how do you know that the next observation you make won't disprove your laws? Remember, in science we technically don't prove anything. We only disprove some ideas, and other ideas become more likely to be true as they go unproven.

"But some of those laws have been tested for so many years..."

But *you* haven't seen that. You are just trusting what other people tell you. Don't listen to your teachers. They don't know what they are talking about.

*Laughter.*

That's just what you've been told, and it's really a conspiracy. It's all been carefully designed to deceive you.

"I know that you need an education to be successful."

It's all an illusion. It's a lie. You don't need an education to be successful.

"Yeah, there are some people who are successful without an education."

True. That's true. However, those people are the rare exception. So, if you are looking at probabilities, you should probably get an education. But, it also depends on what you mean by *success*. If *success* just means making money, there are plenty of illegal ways to do that. But maybe that's not what real success is. Maybe real success has more to do with who and what *you* are than what and how much you *have*.

Ok, we're getting sidetracked. Tell me, what do you know?

"I know that I can die."

Well, maybe. How do you know that there is not more life that comes next? Then you don't really die. You've just changed life form.

"For all we know we died a few years ago and now we are new people."

Right! Reincarnation?

Ultimately, everything that you guys are saying about your bodies and your experiences can be doubted by thinking that maybe you are in the Matrix. But there is an even more radical way of doubting. Rene Descartes, the same guy who invented the Cartesian coordinate plane, the $x\ y$ axis, came up with this doubt. He was a mathematician and a philosopher. So, a double nerd. Descartes said he wanted to see if there was anything he could not doubt. How does he know that he's here right now? How does he know he's not dreaming? Dreaming was like his version of the Matrix. But then he thought that maybe he didn't even have a body. Maybe he is just a mind without a body but with the illusion of a body, and sensory impressions are being pumped into him by some deceiving demon. But when he came down to it, he knew that he was doubting, because even if he is doubting, he knows that he's doubting. He can't doubt the fact that he is doubting, and doubt is a kind of thought. So, he cannot possibly doubt the fact that he is thinking.

*I see a student looking over at one of the quotes on the wall.*
What are you looking at?

"He said that quote, 'I think, therefore I am.'"

Exactly. He knew he was thinking, and he knew that if a thing thinks, then it has to exist. A thing that does not exist cannot think. But, he cannot doubt that he is thinking, so he cannot doubt that he exists. "I think, therefore I am." What it means is, I know I am thinking, so I know that I exist. It may just be as a mind, but he knows that he exists in some way.

Getting past that point is really difficult. He tried, but there is a lot of criticism of him and how he tried to get past knowing that he exists to then knowing that other things exist. A lot of philosophers say that this kind of radical doubt leads to a philosophy called solipsism, which is the philosophy that I am the only thing that exists.

"What?"

Yeah. Solipsism says that all of the rest of you are just an illusion. The only thing I know is that I exist and that I have these impressions.

The question is, then, what does it mean to know something? When we say that we know something, are we talking about this type of certainty? In order for us to know something, do we have to know it in a way that it cannot possibly be doubted? Do we have to come up with all of the other possibilities? Well, we do think through some of the other possibilities, but most of the time we just look at the available evidence and make a judgment from that. Where does the evidence lead? If you try to live your life according to that radical doubt, that is going to be pretty fruitless.

That, by the way, is one of the tests of a philosophy. Can you live it out? Does it make sense in the real world? Because we are dealing with reality, not just making stuff up. We are trying to find out about the nature of reality.

# 16. "Only the Educated are Free"

For today, I have a particular quote from my wall up on the board. True or false? Agree or disagree?

*T or F? Only the educated are free. -Epictetus*

"I think it's false, because if you're uneducated then you are blind to everything and you don't have any worries."
No worries. Hakuna Matata.
"It's complicated. We're not fully educated. But the people who are fully educated have the really high-up jobs. But even they have to pay taxes and do stuff. So, they're not entirely free."
"I wonder if anybody is educated really. There is so much knowledge out there, can anyone be fully educated and have that knowledge? So, how do we define *educated*?"
Ok. What do you think he meant by the word *educated*? Remember the quote, "Many are schooled, but few are educated." So, you need to be careful how you take these words. If by *educated* you mean only having completed a certain level of school and *free* means the ability to make choices out in the real world, that might not be what our friend Epictetus had in mind. Or even the acquisition of knowledge. That is another way we use the word *educated*, but Epictetus probably meant something different.
"I think it's saying that once you've completed college and gotten your master's degree you have more freedom to get the job you want. It's easier to live, and you have more options. As opposed to being raised in a place where you didn't get an education. You don't have the same kind of freedom to do things. You don't have as many options."

"I was going to ask, what is *freedom*?"

Good question! That's important here. Let's put it this way. Are there very highly educated people in prison?

"Yeah."

Right. White collar crimes? So, are they free?

"No."

Not in the sense that we are talking about, like being able to make their own decisions.

"I think different people will think about freedom differently. A person in prison might think that not being in prison is freedom. A person who rents an apartment might think it is freedom to own your own home and not have to answer to a landlord."

Right. The definitions of these terms are really important.

"It's also the freedom to go and pursue what you want to pursue, to learn about different kinds of careers or things in politics that you care about. You're free to make choices in what you want to be."

"If you're educated you have a better idea of how the world works. But if you're not educated and you're poor, you probably have to stick with the same job. You can't get out of that and do something new and better."

Keep in mind, too, that during the time of Epictetus, Ancient Rome, there was not such thing as free, public education. The only schools that existed were tutors to whom you could go if you had money and free time. Only the wealthy received schooling. Free public education didn't come around until the Middle Ages in Europe. The people of that time believed that the mind was a good thing in itself, and that learning was a good thing in itself. So, they started providing free education for everyone, even the poor. It was the monks and the nuns of the Middle Ages who invented public education.

Do you remember the allegory of the cave? The word *education* comes from two Latin words. The prefix *e-* or *ex-* meaning *out* or *out of*, and the word *ducere* which means *to lead*. So *education* means to be lead out. Education has this sense of being lead out of something and into something else. I wonder sometimes if the origin of the word had something to do with the allegory of the cave.

I think what Epictetus had in mind was more this idea of freedom of the mind. Let's say someone has a good education, and he can manipulate a job situation and get the job that he wants, but in his mind, he is a complete slave to whatever the media tells him in the opinions he forms about big questions. Is that person free? Epictetus would say, "no," not in the important way. If someone is very well educated but is addicted to some drug, is he free? No, not in the way Epictetus is talking about. He is a slave to that drug.

So, the word *education* here has more the sense of being able to think for yourself and the freedom to be excellent. He is saying that an educated person can think critically and rationally for himself instead of just accepting whatever society throws at him. *Freedom* is the freedom to recognize truth and live excellently. Freedom is not just being able to do whatever you want, because then you can still be a slave to your passions and your ever-changing wants and desires. Real freedom, for a lot of philosophers, is the ability to reach your full potential. Are you free to seek truth, or are you a slave to the ideas that surround you? Are you free to live excellently, or are you still subject to your passions that carry you from this thing to that, from one thing to the next?

"If you don't know a lot, then you'll just do whatever you're told. You can't think for yourself. But if you're educated you have a better idea of what to do than someone who doesn't know."

"The people who had come out of the cave and seen real dogs and real trees were free because they knew what was really real. But the people down in the cave thought they had an education because they knew the words that corresponded with the shadows. But they only know the word, like the representation of it. They hadn't seen the real thing."

So education is having the ability to think for yourself instead of having your mind controlled by the forces of society around you. Every advertisement you've seen or heard has been carefully constructed by intelligent people to make you think you need that product. *Advertiser voice*: "You need this!" *Gullible voice*: "Oh, yeah! I need that thing!" *Advertiser voice*: "You deserve this!" *Gullible voice*: "Yeah, I deserve that." *Advertiser voice*: "This will make you happy!" *Gullible voice*: "If I only had that, I'd be happy." How often have you heard friends gossiping about somebody else and you just soaked it in. *Gullible voice*: "Oh yeah, that guy's an idiot."

Do a little thought experiment for a second. Imagine that, at the end of the day, you got a list of all the thoughts that went through your head that day. That would be an interesting thing to look at. If you were to look at that list, how many of those thoughts are thoughts that you consciously decided to think about? How many of those things were worth thinking about? How many of those thoughts have you examined to figure out if they are true? As opposed to the number of thoughts that are just mere reactions everything that gets thrown at you through the media, social media, friends, gossip, whatever you hear people talk about. How many of those thoughts did you take a careful look at and say, "This thought is a good one, I'm going to keep it," or, "This is garbage. This one has to go"? Because our words and actions overflow from our thought life. And then if you were to get another list of all the things you said that day...or typed, you know, tweets or whatever. How many of those things were really worth it? Are you really free in the way that you are able to think and see reality and then in what you do and say, or is your whole life just a reaction? And you've been well trained to react certain ways? Even mentally?

So, yes, schooling can be used for education. But schooling is not the same thing as education. You can be very, very well-schooled, and still be a slave mentally.

# 17. What Would you Put in Your Mansion?

This question is not going to seem very philosophical at first, but it is. Just go with it, and then I will tell you how it if philosophical. Got it? Ok. Here we go.

Imagine that for some reason money is not an issue for you. In other words, you had all the money you could want. You win the lottery or something like that. So, you decide to build a mansion, and you can put anything into your mansion that you want. What do you put in your mansion?

"Swimming pool."

Indoor or outdoor?

"Both!"

You could have a whole indoor water theme park.

"Basketball court."

"Movie theater."

"A room size moon walk, bouncy thing."

"I wouldn't get a mansion."

Why not?

"Do you have to build a mansion?"

No, you don't have to, what did you have in mind?

"A big mansion would be too much. I would want something smaller, simpler. A big mansion seems unnecessary."

Ok. I hear you. I would want a smaller place, too. But what would you put it in? Cheap stuff or really nice furniture?

"Nice stuff. I would still put nice stuff in there."

"I would hire an Italian interior designer and have all of my furniture custom made."

"I would have an indoor sand volleyball court."

"Arcade."

And what about all your everyday stuff like furniture, plates, appliances? Would you get junk? Cheap stuff or expensive things?

"Expensive things."

Ok. Now we are going to shift the conversation a bit. How many of you would invite the local garbage company to deposit their garbage in your house? It's got to go somewhere.

"Why would I?"

"No."

"Why are you even asking?"

You'll see. Just stick with me. Ok. And how many of you would invite the sewer company to direct all of their pipes to deposit the sewage into your mansion? So your house is the receptacle for the town sewage.

"That's disgusting."

Yes, I agree. There's a lot of disgusting stuff out there.

But here is the point. You would be very picky, if you had the choice, about what you put into your mansion. You would want only the best, the nicest stuff.

*I say the next sentence and question slowly and with emphasis.*

Your mind is a palace, worth far more than any mansion you could buy. What do you put into your mind?

*Audible groans.*

Think about everything that you have watched, looked at, seen, listened to, said and done in the last 24 hours. How much of it was garbage? And some of it you don't seek out purposefully. It just gets thrown at you through the various forms of media. But even then, how much of that stuff do you allow to live in your mind? Garbage, or priceless stuff? Only the best?

*Quietly:* "It's all garbage."

"Well, what do you define as garbage? What exactly? What if you want to go on YouTube and you want to watch whatever you want to watch? It's just entertainment. It makes you happy."

Right. What kind of happy does it make you?

"Short-term, I guess."

So, the question that I asked back to you is a philosophical question. I was addressing the nature of real happiness and the different types of happiness that we experience. That's part of the process of philosophy. What is the real kind of happiness we are looking for, and that depends on the basic structure of reality and the nature you have as a human being. For example. If you are nothing but a body without any soul or anything like that, then your greatest good is probably just physical pleasure. If you are a body soul unity or there is some soul component to you, then maybe the soul is more important. You should pursue health of soul instead of just health of body. And so you should seek out forms of entertainment that are going to contribute to the health of your soul, seeking out whatever is going to help you reach your full potential.

But even answering the question about what is garbage and what is the good stuff, that depends on these deep questions about the nature of reality and the nature of what it means to be a human. I have that quote on the wall, the one in Greek, but it means, "Know Thyself." It was inscribed above the door of the Delphic Oracle, and it inspired Socrates to philosophize. It doesn't mean to take a personality test to discover if you're an introvert or an extrovert or know that you have a dream of becoming a singer or know that you enjoy watching comedies. That's not what it is talking about: your preferences and your personality. It means to know your essence and your nature as a human. If you can answer that question, then that will help you answer every other question in your life. You have two choices for your entertainment. If you have a clear picture of *what* it is that you are and what is good for you, then the best choice will be much clearer. But if you haven't answered that fundamental question about yourself, then you just pick whatever you feel like or whatever happens to be most appealing at the moment.

Philosophy helps you to evaluate all the things in your house and decide what is worth keeping and what has to be taken out to the curb. And then philosophy can act as a doorman and decide what gets in and what does not. It is a way of sifting through all the various ideas that come knocking on your door throughout the day to let in what is true and good and beautiful and to keep out what is false and bad and ugly.

And this is not easy because you have lived for sixteen or seventeen years just letting everything in. I didn't start thinking this way until later in college. A lot of garbage gets stored away in the mind, habits are formed, and it is really tough to change all of that. We have been conditioned to think a certain way, but we should question even those ways we have been conditioned to think.

# 18. The Meaning of Life

The question we are going to discuss today is a very common question, but you might not realize that it is actually a philosophical question. So, here it is: What is the meaning of life? Close your laptops! And it's not playing video games. I can tell you that!

*Laughter.*

"To be or not to be."

Whoa! Quoting *Hamlet* over here.

"It's the universe experiencing itself."

The universe experiencing itself. How do you know?

"I just know. You're going to have to take my word for it."

Well, I guess that settles it. Other ideas? What is the meaning of life?

"To achieve greatness!"

Ok. That's interesting. What is greatness?

"It's the American Dream!"

"Wife, kids, house, lawn, white picket fence and an American flag."

Wife, kids, house, lawn, white picket fence and an American flag? That's the meaning of life?

"Yeah."

What about for non-Americans? What is their meaning of life?

"To do that, but...just...what their version is..."

Just a different flag?

"I don't know. Now it just sounds stupid. I was only thinking about Americans at the time."

Well, ok. This is good. This is an important step in philosophy. We have these initial impressions and thoughts.

But we want to take those and examine them because there is probably something there that is right. There is usually some aspect of that that makes sense, but we have to sort through it.

"I think the meaning of life is to be happy. To feel needed by your kids and your spouse if that's what makes you happy. I feel like when I am dying I will know that I had a really good time, so it doesn't matter."

That was great. There were two things there. First you said to be happy, and then you gave a definition of happiness. But then you changed it at the end. The first way you described happiness was having a family and kids and being needed by them, serving them. But then you changed it at the end to having fun.

"Yeah."

Or maybe being needed *is* having fun.

"Right."

So if a friend is getting drunk on the weekends and says he's having fun, you would tell him that's not really fun. Being needed by your kids is fun.

*Laughter.*

"But that's not why you're doing it. You're going to have fun in the outcome, but you're doing it. At some point, what you're doing right now is going to make you happy. Like, I wouldn't be here right now if it wasn't required for me to get a good job. No one would be here."

Unfortunately, I think you're right. Ok. Other ideas?

"I think it means doing what you need to do to survive and live. So, you go to school because you need that to get a good job and live. That's how you make a family."

"What if you can't have kids?"

"Then your life is meaningless."

"You can adopt kids!"

I've adopted kids. Did you guys know this? I have four adopted kids.

"Yes, we knew this."

"How many kids do you have?"

Seven.

"Seven!?"

Yes. Seven. It's not easy, but it's worth it. Other thoughts?

"Life has no meaning."

Ok. How do you know?

"I don't know. Well, because everyone gives a different answer, and everyone has different things they live for. There is no correct answer."

That may be true, but how do you know there is no correct answer?

"It's different for everybody."

"Some people like sleeping. Some people like singing. Some people like other things. We are all different."

That's what people enjoy doing. That's not the same as the meaning of life.

"It's science. We come here, and we die. There is no meaning."

Science actually can't tell us anything about meaning.

"Exactly. Science tells us there is no meaning."

No, no. It's not that science tells us there is no meaning. It's that science cannot tell us if there is meaning or not. This is a philosophical question, not a scientific one.

"People have different personalities. Everybody's meaning of life is different."

How many serious thinkers have you consulted on this question?

"One. You."

Well, I haven't told you anything...yet.

"Do you know?"

I am convinced of an answer, yes. Having studied philosophy and read a lot of books from some of the great minds of the past, I have come to some definite conclusions. I think there is a good answer to that question, and a really beautiful one, too. I won't give you all the details here and now, but I can give you a few summary statements.

"I think it is to live your life."

What do you mean? As long as you're living you are living your life.

"No. What I mean is to live your life to the fullest."

So, maybe that is the meaning of life. To live your life to the fullest. But! Here is the question: what does it mean to live life to the fullest? For example, is living an entertaining life the same thing as living a fulfilling life?

"No."

"You can entertain yourself all the time and accomplish nothing."

"It's up to them. If that's what they want to do and that's their purpose, then that's the meaning of their life. It's different for everyone."

But aren't you saying that living life to the fullest is the same for everyone, but that is just going to look different for everyone?

"Right."

Most philosophers would argue that either there is an intrinsic meaning for everyone, even if it looks different for each individual *or* there is no meaning at all.

"What do you think, Mr. D? What is the meaning of life?"

Well, I will give you some hints, but I won't give my full answer. You can consult my other books or my YouTube channel for that. But, here are a couple of different "secular" ways of putting it. One way of putting it is this: to love and to be loved. Another way of saying it is to reach your full potential. Matthew Kelly, an author I like, has a phrase that describes it: to become the best version of yourself. Those are all different ways of saying the same thing. And I agree that it comes down to living your life to the fullest, and it will look different for everyone, but there are some essential characteristics that are the same. There is more to it, but this exercise is to make you think.

Once again, even though I haven't given you a clear-cut answer, I want you to know that there have been serious, well-thought out answers to this question. And they are not hard to find. But it takes some work. What could be more important to find out about, though?

# 19. Where do Your Rights Come From?

Today's question is where do your rights come from? People argue for equal rights. They say, "We have these rights! We want our rights!" There are a lot of arguments about who has what rights. So, it's important to get to the foundation of the idea. If we can figure out the basis of rights in the first place, then that should be able to help us figure out what rights we have and which rights we don't. People say, "The government is not recognizing my rights!" Why? Why do you have those rights? How do you know you have those rights? Maybe you're just talking about something you want but you're attaching the label *rights.*

"The Constitution."

The Constitution, right? That's the first answer people give almost all the time. Our rights come from the Constitution. So, what about people who don't live in the United States? Do they have rights? And, did people have rights before the Constitution was written?

"People who don't live in the United States are given rights by the Constitutions of their own countries."

Ok. Well, according to the Constitutions of some countries, some people do not have the right to an education. And this is a reality. Is it true, then, that those people do not have the right to an education? Or, do they have the right to an education, but their government doesn't recognize it?

Here is another problem. If your rights come from the Constitution, then it makes *no* sense to argue that you have some rights that are not in the Constitution. If your rights only come from the Constitution, then it is impossible to have any rights that are not recognized there. So, how can you argue that you have rights that are not in the Constitution? That makes no sense.

"I think that when we create some legal document saying that we have these rights, what we are saying is that we believe in the legitimacy of the government and we believe that we have these rights. But if we start to doubt that political structure or there is some social change, then we can start over and rewrite our rights."

So, there are certain rights that are given to us by the government. The question is, do we have any rights independently of the government or the Constitution. For example, the Declaration of Independence says that we have certain *inalienable* rights, rights that cannot be taken away from us. In other words, we have these rights whether the government recognizes them or not. Where does that come from? Why?

"I think it's just because we are alive that we have the right to life. Just living is the reason we have the right to live."

But why? Why is it that being alive gives you the right to life? And what are rights in the first place? Can you look at rights under a microscope? Can you get quantitative data on rights? What does a right look like? Is it shaped like an amoeba?

"The founders of our country wrote that we are endowed by our Creator with rights. So, in their view, our rights came from God."

"I think our rights are just agreed upon by society. So, if someone is living alone, then he doesn't have any rights because he doesn't have a society. In some countries where people don't have the right to an education, they don't have that right because they haven't agreed on that as a society. Here in our country, that is what we have agreed to. Right and wrong is just what we agree to."

In that case, is it not *intrinsically* wrong to murder an innocent person?

"It's wrong, but it's not right."

It's wrong but it's not right? What do you mean?

"It's wrong to murder someone, but it's not wrong without society."

So, it's not *really* wrong to just kill someone?

"I don't think *wrong* and *not right* are the same thing."

"Is this a question of moral rights or people rights?"

Good question. If we do have intrinsic rights, it is certainly tied to our morality. So, you might say that it is wrong to kill somebody because they have the right to live. They have the right to their own freedom. Or at least as stated by the authors of the Declaration of Independence, they have the right to life, and it is wrong to violate that right.

Or, not to get too graphic, but go even further than that. Think about abuse or something like that. Does a child have a right to not be physically abused? Does a woman have a right to not be raped? If we are talking about intrinsic rights, we are really talking about codes of conduct.

"I think our rights are given to us by society. Because for a long time people thought slavery was ok, for thousands of years. So, some people didn't have the right to freedom. But now we agree that slavery is not ok, so everyone has the right to freedom. And this goes on all the time in a lot of different areas. We see a lot of progress in history, and there is progress in rights."

There is certainly a lot of change, but is change the same thing as progress? Progress implies that you are moving towards something good. More developed means that you are getting closer to some standard of development. If there is no ultimate standard, then we are not any better or worse than other societies, no more or less developed; we are also not any more or less progressed; we are just different.

"Well, we improve over time. As humans, we are improving all the time, and that ought to be commended. Like, we don't do human sacrifice anymore."

So, by *improve* you mean *make better*.

"Yeah."

Are some moral standards better intrinsically or just in your thought?

"Um..."

Because, again, if you are saying that there is no ultimate *intrinsic* standard built into reality somehow, then – you said, "it ought to be commended." Well, why? Not if there isn't some standard. Maybe because you like it more, so you'll commend it. But that doesn't mean that it *ought* to be commended. If there is no ultimate standard, then there is no such thing as progress; there's just change. Wearing a blue shirt today is not progress from wearing a red shirt yesterday, because wearing a blue shirt is not necessarily better than wearing a red shirt. It's just different. Human sacrifice, no human sacrifice; one is not necessarily better than the other. It is just different. It's just what those societies have agreed on. *And* the human sacrifice ended when people came in from other countries and saw what was happening. They said, "That is terrible! You shouldn't be doing that! These people have rights." Was that oppression? How dare they impose their own views on the people and their cultural practices of human sacrifice. *Or*, were they right? Was it really wrong to sacrifice fellow humans by ripping their hearts out while they were still living?

"We just read something in another class that says when we talk about what people's rights should be, we are talking about people and other creatures within our circles. So, as we have come into contact with other societies and there is globalization, the whole world is now in a common agreement or is coming to one. In those times, those people were not in contact with each other. So, when we say people should have some rights, we are talking about what we have the ability to influence. In the past it wasn't better or worse. It's just that our moral circles have changed. And as we learn more about artificial intelligence and the brains of other animals, we should reconsider what we include in our moral circle."

Interesting. So, that last part of what you said was holding up brain structure as a reason for granting rights. Why should brain structure be a basis for rights?

"Because they are more similar to humans. We consider things like us to have the same rights as us."

Ok. But if there are no intrinsic standards in the first place, why do we care about similarities? After all, the humans who were sacrificed were more similar to us in brain structure, in fact, the same, than other animals. They were other human beings. They really were of the same species as us.

Also, as you were speaking, you said *should*. There is no unqualified *should* if there are no intrinsic rights or standards.

As I talk about these things and ask if it really not wrong to murder, rape, wipe out whole races of people, I can see people cringe. As philosophers, we want to ask if our reaction is some really important evidence that there is a standard, or is our reaction just a result of our cultural brainwashing and there really is no standard? If you deny the standard altogether, then you have to live that out as if there really are no standards. Remember, we are dealing with reality, not making stuff up. So our philosophy has to be something that we can live. Philosophy should make sense of the world and our experience, not explain them away. If you have some idea in your mind that is impossible for you to live out, then you are probably not thinking about reality. We are not writing fiction. Philosophy is about reality.

So, if we say that there are no ultimate standards or intrinsic rights, then that undercuts a lot of our experience as humans, what we think and feel. When we hear or read about some terrible thing that people have done, and we get angry and want to condemn someone or at least their actions, we have to hold back and remind ourselves that it's not really wrong, just different, if there are no standards. As philosophers we want our philosophy to be consistent.

We have to wrap this up now and get to some physics, but I want you to know that philosophers have written about topics like the basis of our rights and standards of morality for hundreds of years. There are good, well thought out arguments on different sides. I don't want you walking away with the impression that there are no answers just because we haven't come to a resolution here. Philosophy takes time. One of the quotes on my wall says that there is no short road to riches in philosophy. The important thing is to keep seeking and asking good questions because it's worth it.

# 20. Do You Push the Button?

Let's do Philosophy Friday! Close your laptops and other such things because I have a deal for you.

"A deal?"

Yes. Here is the deal. I have a button. Not really, I am just pretending, there is no button in reality, but it's part of this hypothetical situation. Anyway, I have this button, and all you have to do is push this button. If you push the button, you get a billion dollars, but...

*I pause dramatically. They look excited but hesitant.*

"But...?"

"Yeah, what's the 'but'?"

...when you push that button, someone who you do not know nor ever will know or find out about, will die suddenly and painlessly. Do you push that button?

*Slight chaos ensues.*

"Yeah I push that button!"

"No!"

*Some students make dramatic "pushing the button" motions.*

Ok! Hold on! One at a time. Raise your hand. Tell me yes or no and why.

"Well, yeah, I push the button because they are going to die painlessly, and then I could donate half of that money to charity. So, the good that money can do worldwide will offset the death of just one person."

"Offset!?"

*Laughter.*

Now, you *could* donate that money, but *would* you?

"I mean some... a bit."

*Laughter.*

"They might have the same ability to press the button, and I wouldn't want to die from that. So, I wouldn't do it."

"I wouldn't because people who win the lottery always go crazy."

"But maybe it's someone who deserves to die or someone who's about to die anyway."

"But maybe not! Maybe it's just some kid running around on the playground all happy and then splat, he's dead."

Is there a difference?

"But you don't know, and I would have to live with the guilt of that."

Ok. Let me change the situation. I am going to turn the tables on you now. What if I said that someone else, somewhere in the world is being offered this deal, but the person who will die is the family member you care about most. Do you want them to push that button?

"No way."

"I would say my goodbyes."

"I would buy them really good life insurance."

That's going to look fishy. You buy good life insurance for them and then they die?

*Laughter.*

What if somehow you knew that the person who pushes the button is going to donate all the money to charity. Would be ok with that?

"If they cured cancer with that money, then, yes, I would be ok with that. I would die. I would die for that."

No, not you. Your closest family member.

"I would see if it's ok with them first."

Ok. So, here's the lesson. What we are talking about is an ethical question. Most of the time, when faced with questions like this, we don't stop to think about the basis for making a decision, we just try to make a decision. But in philosophy, we want to get to the foundation, the "Why?" at the bottom of making decisions. And there are three basic, underlying philosophies in ethics. The first two are very common today, and the other one is hardly known at all except among philosophers.

The first one is utilitarianism. This is based on the idea that what makes an action right is the end result. You look ahead and figure out what choices will lead to the most good for the most people, and those are the actions you take. The ends justify the means. So, even if you have to do something we normally think is "bad," that is actually the right thing to do because actions are judged by the result. Even if it means killing someone or a whole group of people, as long as the good that will result is better than what would happen without killing them, then that is the right thing to do. This, of course, assumes that we can figure out what will happen and that we know exactly what "good" is.

The second general philosophy of ethics is universal law ethics. It is sometimes known as deontology. This philosophy is based on the idea that there is some moral law or set of laws that you have to follow, and that's it. If your actions obey that law, then those are right. If your actions disobey that law, then your actions are wrong. Immanuel Kant gave a version of this philosophy. I know this sounds like the kind of morality we hear about in religion, but a lot of traditional religions actually don't have a universal law as a basis for morals. Some of the older ones fall into the third philosophy.

Most of us today operate under one or both of those first two philosophies, whether we realize it or not. You use some basis for making your decisions, even if you don't know it. So it is really important to figure it out because it can make a big difference in how you make decisions.

The third philosophy is one that very few people know about today, but it was *the* dominant philosophy among the great thinkers in the Ancient and Medieval worlds. It is based on the idea that humans have a particular nature, and that it is right to act in harmony with that nature and it is wrong to act contrary to that nature. It is sometimes called natural law ethics because it is based on the idea that the nature of what it is to be a human is the source of the law.

Let me give you an illustration. Let's imagine that someone finds a guitar, but he has never seen a guitar before, and he doesn't know what it's for. So, he takes it home and uses it for construction. He uses it to hammer in some nails, to drive some screws, to do some painting. He uses it as a crowbar to take down some drywall. What is going to happen to that guitar?

*By this time my students are looking at me like I am crazy, as they often do.*

"It will break."

Right! It will break or be badly damaged. But, what if the guitar is placed in the hands of a guitarist? It will produce beautiful music.

In the same way, if you "use" yourself in a way contrary to your nature, you will damage yourself. But if you make decisions according to what you are as a human, then your life can be beautiful music. The worst part about the damage, though, is that the more you damage yourself the less you know you are damaged. Your understanding is a part of what you are, and if you are damaged, then your understanding is damaged. Remember the quote from Plato? "The really damaging thing about stupidity is its self-satisfaction." But if you act according to your nature, you become a better and better version of yourself.

So, in answer to the question about the button, the utilitarian would probably say to push the button and use the money, or at least some of it, to do some amount of good to "offset" the death. That would be the right thing to do for a utilitarian, probably. The universal law ethicist would most likely say not to push the button because it is wrong to kill. Most likely, because it depends on what the law is. Maybe the law says it is not wrong to kill. The natural law ethicist would first have to figure out if it is in accord with the nature of what it means to be human to push a button that kills someone and get a lot of money, and then act based on what he figures out.

There is an important application point for you all, though, that I want to point out. Obviously, you don't really have the opportunity to push a button that kills someone for a billion dollars, but every day you have the decision to push a button...

*I take out and hold up my cell phone.*

...that could kill someone socially or emotionally or kill someone's self-esteem. And for what? A billion dollars? No. A few likes. Some shares. Getting people to laugh. A retweet. This question might turn out to be more applicable that it might look at first.

But the important thing is to examine the underlying philosophies and figure out which one is true. Then you will have a basis for making all the rest of your decisions in life.

# 21. Why You Should Cheat

Happy Philosophy Friday!

"Oh yeah! Philosophy Friday!"

That's right. We are going to do some philosophizing at the start of class here today. We are going to talk about something that you may have done or you know people are doing on a regular basis, and that is cheating. Why cheat? Why should you cheat? I know you are often told why you shouldn't cheat. Let's talk about why you *should* cheat for a little while.

"Cheating...like in school or in a relationship?"

Good question. Cheating in school. Tests and quizzes, copying papers, homework. That sort of thing. Cheating in a relationship is a whole other discussion, though related, believe it or not. So, why cheat in school?

"It's the easy way out."

It's the easy way out of what?

"So I don't have to think."

Why do you not want to think?

"Because I'm lazy."

So, why be lazy?

"Because that's the easy thing."

We already said that. So we are back to the easy thing now. Why do the easy thing?

"Because it's not as hard."

Yes, that's what easy means.

*Laughter.*

But why do that?

"Why not?"

Well, why do you not want to work hard?

"Because I'm lazy."

93

Why are you lazy?

"Because things can be hard and we don't want to do them."

Right, we've been over that. So, how did you become lazy?

"I don't think you are a lazy person. I think you are just lazy at times."

"That makes you lazy."

"I don't think so. I think it's just inconsistent."

So, lazy towards some things?

"Lazy towards homework. I never do homework."

"I don't like to do the dishes, so I don't. Then my parents do them."

So, it seems like you just do what you've trained yourself to do. You do what you feel like doing.

"Yeah."

Is what you feel like doing always the best thing to do?

"No."

Alright. Let's think about cheating then. Instead of deciding whether we feel like it or not, let's think about some good reasons to cheat, because feeling like it is not a good reason. We just went over that, right?

"To get a good grade."

"So you don't fail."

Right. And this all concerns you directly. It's a good thing to think about. Why get a good grade?

"Get into a good school?"

Is that a question?

*Laughter.*

"Ok. To get into a good school."

Said with confidence. That's better. But why get into a good school?

"So you can get a job."

Why get a job? Can you get a good job without having gone to a good school?

"Yes!"

Ok. Let's review. We said cheat to get good grades so you can get into a good school so you can get a job...

"Get a *good* job."

What makes a good job?

"Something you enjoy."

"Making good money. More money than another job."

Ok. You're looking for enjoyment. Are there jobs that you could potentially enjoy that don't make good money?

"Yeah. *A lot* of jobs."

Making good money, then, is not the same thing as enjoying your job. So why have a job that makes more money?

"So you can do more things in your life."

Like what?

"Support your family."

Can you support your family with a lower paying job? Look, I'm a teacher, and I have seven kids. I am not raking in the big bucks, but I can support my family.

"You can be more comfortable if you make more money probably."

Ah! Comfort!

"Well, around certain holidays you won't be as stressed because you will have money to spend."

Does having more money make you less stressed?

"Yes."

"Actually..."

Let's look statistically. Look at the people who make the most money. Are they the least stressed?

"No! Because their job is very stressful."

Right! Listen to this. Think about it. Your generation has had more comfort and convenience than any other generation in history, but depression and anxiety rates for your generation are the highest they have ever been in history. Therefore, comfort and convenience are not the same thing as satisfaction or happiness.

"Well, it depends on the person. Because they might be some people's happiness."

It depends on the person. Great point. Back to cheating now. When you cheat, what kind of person are you turning yourself into?

"Lazy."

"You're lying to yourself."

You are reinforcing laziness. You are also reinforcing deception because you are becoming a person who deceives. Does that sound like the kind of person that will experience real happiness in life?

"If that's his happiness."

Being deceptive and lazy is his happiness?

"Maybe if he wants to be like that."

Even if he might want to be like that, is that going to result in real happiness? Think about those qualities, and then think about what a truly joyful person is like.

"If he likes what he's doing."

Ultimately, it depends on the type of person that you make yourself into. So you need to ask yourself that question: what does it look like to be the fullest and best version of myself? And then take the actions that are going to lead to that.

Human beings are interesting things. This computer is a computer whether it likes it or not. And it is what it is purely as a result of external forces. It is not self-determining. Human beings, on the other hand, become what they become as a direct result of the choices they make. We are influenced by our surroundings, but we can make whatever happens to us into a better thing or a worse thing depending on how we react to it. No matter what happens to you, you have the choice of how to respond. And the way that you respond will determine who you are, the kind of person you are, at the end of it. Not that it's easy to make different choices once you have formed certain habits. Anyone can try to start making different choices any time, but the sooner you start making different choices, the easier it will be to break old habits and form new ones and start reaching your full potential. I wish someone had told me about this and made me start thinking about this stuff when I was a teenager.

"Did you ever cheat?"

Yeah. Once that I remember.

"What was it?"

It was a history quiz, and it wasn't worth it. It was more work than it would have been to study, and I was so worried about getting caught. I never did it again.

But I realize that you guys are facing more pressure than I was. That doesn't justify cheating, but I realize it's not easy. My parents didn't put a ton of pressure on me. My friends and I were not super competitive about grades and class rank. I got good grades, but I didn't have the world breathing down my neck. Maybe if I had started cheating earlier, it would have come more naturally, but I am glad that I have not turned myself into a person who cheats. Believe me, I have enough of my own problems and bad habits. I don't need to add that one.

And so, that's the best reason to cheat: to turn yourself into the kind of person who cheats. Why should you cheat? To become a cheater. Any other goal you have for cheating could be attained in some other way, and those other achievements will be experienced by a person who cheats or a person who doesn't. The real question is whether the habit of cheating is included in the full potential of a human being.

# 22. Can Money Buy Love?

Happy Philosophy Friday! Today we are going to discuss a question that I save for Valentine's Day. Of course, it has to do with love.

"Aw."

I know. It's so sweet.

*Laughter.*

So, the question is this: can money buy love? What do you think?

"Yes."

"In a way."

Ok. You said yes, and you said in a way. First we are going hear the yes answer.

"That's right! You wait your turn!"

Not a lot of love right now. Ok, why?

"Because there are certain things that you like doing. If you have money, you can buy those things or pay to do those things. I love cars, and if I had enough money, I would buy new cars all the time, and I would love my life."

There are people who have done that. A lot of them go into depression because it doesn't make them really happy.

But let me ask you this: is money buying you love or the thing that you love?

"The thing that I love."

So it's not buying you love.

"Right."

Ok. So now back to money buying love in a way. Let's hear that.

"Well...I mean. Like gold diggers."

You mean women who go out with guys and marry them because they are rich?

"You could be ugly and have a ton of money, and girls will want to be with you."

Are you buying love, then? Does she really love you?

"Eh…good point."

"Love is not a physical thing. It's just a feeling."

Love is a feeling. Then can you buy a drug to give you the feeling? Maybe we can invent a love drug.

"But that's still not the feeling."

It's a synthetic thing? It's not natural?

"Right."

Ok. Well, this is good. What just happened here? You identified what love is. You said it's a feeling. Whether that is true or false is a separate question, but saying what the word means is extremely important. Definition of terms is the most important part of any discussion. What is this thing we are talking about in the first place? You said love is a feeling. Great. Now we can figure out if you can buy that feeling. Awesome.

But we can go back and discuss whether love is just a feeling. One of the ways we can look at words is how they are used in our everyday language. It was said earlier, "I love cars." How else do we use that word? Just give me examples of how you use that word in a sentence.

"If someone let's me go ahead of them in the lunch line, I am like, 'Oh, thank you! I love you.'"

"I love my mom and dad."

"I love my friends."

"I love this school."

"I love life."

"People say 'I love you' to their boyfriend or girlfriend."

Right. Ok. So, do you love cars, people who do nice things for you, your parents, and your boyfriend and girlfriend in the same way? Are we using the same word in the same way in all those different sentences? Is your love for your significant other the same kind of love you have for your mom?

"No!"

There are different kinds of love. This is very important. That is a different thing! But when we use the word "love," one thing or another comes to mind. This is the issue of definitions. This is a problem. We have one word and all of these different things that it can mean. This can lead to a lot of confusion. What may end up happening is that the word comes to mean nothing at all. It will get spread too thin and mean so many things that ultimately it loses its meaning.

In the mean time, there is a lot of foolishness about this word, and people say a lot of silly things about love because we haven't taken the time to carefully think through exactly what we mean by the word in each of these contexts. As opposed to the Ancient Greeks. They actually had four different words, and we would translate all of those words as "love."

One of them is *storge*.

*As I talk about these words I write them on the board.*

Storge love is the natural family bond between family members. So, when you say that you love your mom and dad, you are talking about storge love. They had a specific name for the love that exists between parents and children, between brothers and sisters.

"I storge my mom."

Right! If you were speaking in Ancient Greek, that's the word you would use.

Another word for love is phileo. This is the love between friends. It stems from having a common interest. One image that has been used to visualize this type of love is two people standing shoulder to shoulder looking at something they both find interesting. The common interest brings them together. You have this kind of love automatically with anyone you are in a club with or on a sports team with. This is also the word in *philosophy* that means love. Philosophy means the love of wisdom. Also, Philadelphia is the city of brotherly love, right? Well, that's what the name means. Phileo means love, and adelphos is the Greek word for brother. Brotherly love. Phil-adelphia.

The next word is eros. This is romantic love. This is the kind of love I have with my wife or that you may have with your significant other. We get our word erotic from this word, but it doesn't just mean sexual love. This word also has a broader definition of desire sometimes. I just read a book recently where the author identifies eros as the natural human desire for what is good and beautiful.

The fourth word is agape. This love is the self-sacrificial willing of the good of the other. It is when you want what is good for the other person and you are willing to do whatever it takes for the person to have that good. If you are in a relationship with someone, and you are not sure if they have this kind of love for you, ask yourself if they would be willing to make sacrifices for you. They may desire you, as in eros, but are they willing to sacrifice for you because they really care for you, as in agape?

There used to be another English word for this kind of love: charity. But language changes and charity has come to mean serving the poor. We have lost a bit of our understanding of this kind of love as a result, unfortunately. Our language forms our culture, and our culture forms our language. If we lose the meaning of a word, then we lose that understanding of that thing as a culture. This is the point Orwell was making in *1984* with newspeak. Have you guys read that?

"Some of us. Some English classes read it."

Ok. You should all read it. It's scary.

I should point out that there are different nuances to these words, too, depending on context. It is not always so cut and dry, but at least they had four different words for four different things, as opposed to us who have one word for so many different things.

So, definition of terms is important! Especially important when it comes to important topics. There is a lot of confusion about love. Next time you hear a slogan or headline or something, ask yourself about the definition of love. Very few popular sayings and memes come with definition of terms afterwards.

# 23. Fallacies: Equivocation

Let's get started. One of the basic things anyone has to learn in philosophy is logic. You might think that it is a basic thing everyone should learn, but apparently not since it is not included in most high school curricula. I have heard multiple college professors lament the fact that high schools don't teach a full course in logic. Math professors and philosophy professors wish you were taught at least a half a course on logic.

"Why?"

Because they have to read papers that students write, and sometimes the logic of the arguments is obscenely bad.

The closest thing you get to logic is probably in Geometry when you study proofs. You learn about if-then statements and a few different forms of an argument on your way to proving a theorem. Maybe you learn about a few other logical fallacies in English class, but that's about it.

There are a few very common fallacies that I think you should know about. A fallacy is a mistake in thinking or making an argument. We have already looked at the fallacy of self-refuting statements a couple of times. Do you remember? The statements "There is no truth" and "Science is the only way to know what is true" turned out to be self-refuting. So, we are going to spend today and the next two Philosophy Fridays discussing three common fallacies. Once I point them out to you, you will immediately recognize them, but you will be amazed how often people commit these fallacies if you pay attention.

On the board I have an argument from a textbook on logic which I actually recommend if you want to learn logic. It's called

*Socratic Logic* by Peter Kreeft. He presents this argument as an example of this logical fallacy. This type of argument is called a syllogism. There are two premises and a conclusion. Here, the two premises are two famous quotes from two famous people in history. When you put them together, you get this conclusion. But, in this syllogism there is a logical fallacy. Let's see if you can find it.

*This is what is written on the board:*

*"Knowledge is power." —Francis Bacon*
*"Power tends to corrupt." -Lord Action*
*Therefore, knowledge tends to corrupt.*

So, what is wrong with this argument? According to this argument, I am corrupting you. All of school, since we are giving you knowledge, is just a process of corruption. But, that doesn't seem to make sense. Therefore, let's see if we can find the problem with this argument.

"Well, the first is like mind power, and the other is real power."

Ok. Can you give an example of that? Is mind power not real power?

"Well...real power has influence. It can do things. Mind power is just knowing things."

"I think the power that comes from knowledge is like power over your circumstances. But the power that tends to corrupt is like absolute power, like what a monarch has. Power over people."

"I think it depends on what you do with your knowledge. Some people use their knowledge for good things. Some people use their knowledge to cure cancer, but some people use knowledge to take advantage of people."

Yeah. Good. You are on the right track. What's happening here is the manipulation of this term *power*. It is being used in two different senses. One way of seeing this is by recognizing who these people are. Francis Bacon was a philosopher who is credited in part with developing and promoting the scientific method and reliance on experimentation. He was at the end of a long line of philosophers in the Middle Ages who said that experimentation is a good way to do science and gain knowledge about the natural world. He is talking about scientific knowledge. If you know about your circumstances, then you can act appropriately, just like you said.

Lord Action was a historian. He was talking about governmental power. Monarchs turning into tyrants. When some people have power over other people, that tends to corrupt. He doesn't say that it necessarily will, but it has that tendency.

"That's like the media. The media has a lot of power."

Yeah, I think you are right. And to your point, here is a little story about the power of the media. I went to a concert at the New Jersey Symphony Orchestra a few years ago, and they were going to be performing a new piece. So, the composer was on the stage before the performance fielding questions, and someone asked him what it took to be successful as a composer, because this guy has done well. He said that having talent and knowing people are both important, but then he made an interesting comment. He said that the media plays an inordinately large role in telling the public who they should like. I thought this was fascinating, because the media had obviously been good to him. But he recognized that the media has incredible power in telling people who they should like, what causes are noble or not, which ideas are good or not. How many opinions do you hold simply because the media has portrayed to you that those are the opinions you should hold? So, watch out for that. Remember, your mind is a palace. Pay attention to what goes in there.

Anyway, in the argument, the term "power" changes definition halfway through. That is not allowed. If you want to say A is B, and B is C, therefore A is C, you can't change the meaning of B from the first to the second premise. That word has multiple senses. When this changing of the term happens, it is called equivocation. Equivocation is the name of the fallacy when someone changes the definition of the term in the middle of the argument and manipulates it to get the conclusion they want.

This goes back to last week. Do you remember? We talked about love. This fallacy happens all the time when people talk about love because the definition is so vague and changeable. But when you think about it, you realize that it's true. Even young children get this. My son once said that he loved chocolate. I was joking around, and I said, "Oh yeah? Well then why don't you marry it?" He replied, "No, Dad. Not that kind of love."

*Laughter.*

It is very easy to equivocate with the term love. Definition of terms is so important. This would be a really important thing to master for any of you on the debate team.

This is a really common fallacy, especially in a society where we don't take the time to define our terms. We have slogans, headlines, sound bites, memes. None of these are really good for people who want to think critically, but a good critical thinker will look at these phrases and ask, "What exactly are we talking about here?"

It is important to realize, though, that just because there is a fallacy does not mean the conclusion is false. The conclusion may still be true, but the presence of a fallacy means that the argument does not work.

# 24. Fallacies: Chronological Snobbery

Happy Friday! Today we are continuing our Philosophy Friday mini-series on logic and logical fallacies. We are trying to learn to think critically and clearly. One of the ways we try to do that is to identify logical fallacies, mistakes people make in their arguments so that the conclusion does not follow from the premises. There is an argument on the board, and the argument is ridiculous. I made it that way in order to highlight what the problem is.

So, here is the argument: the idea that slavery is wrong developed in the 1600s and has nothing to do with our modern times. Therefore, the idea that slavery is wrong is false.

What is wrong with this argument? It claims that a certain idea belongs to another time period, and therefore it is wrong.

"The slave trade is still present in the world today."

True. You're right. But the argument is identifying the idea with a certain time period. That idea belonged to people of that time period. We are people of a different time period, and we get to make up our own ideas.

This fallacy has to do with saying an idea is wrong because it belongs to some other time period. But, that does not make an idea wrong. And you hear this fallacy all the time. Unfortunately, it is not spelled out like this. Usually it is posed as a conversation stopper. Here is how you normally hear it: "That is so old-fashioned." If people say that something is old-fashioned, then they might be right, but that doesn't make it false. That doesn't make it not true. Just because an idea is old, doesn't mean that it's not true.

Here is the other part of this. It is important to realize that even our age will one day be old. A few hundred years from now, people might look back at us and say, "Oh, those people from the early 21ˢᵗ century. They believed blah, blah, blah. They were idiots."

The most common area where you hear this fallacy is with respect to morality. "That is so old-fashioned." "That is out of date." "Be more progressive." Well, what does time have to do with the truth about some proposition? If an idea is false, it's not false because it's old...or new for that matter. It's false on some other grounds.

The name of this fallacy is one of the best names, if not the best name, for a fallacy: chronological snobbery. It means you are a snob because of your time period. People are only appealing to what is new. "It's new, therefore it's true." That's bad logic, and that's a bad argument. When we spell it out like this, it is easy to see. But when it is hidden in a sound bite or a statement of ridicule, it is tough to recognize and can have a strong emotional affect.

"It could also go the other way. I think that the fact that the idea has been around since the 1600s shows that it's a good idea."

Right. And that is actually the reverse of chronological snobbery. Someone might say in support of an idea, "The Ancient Greeks believed blah, blah, blah." It is like saying that an idea is *old*, therefore it is true. We contradict ourselves sometimes as a society. We appeal to progress and modernity, and we say that some ideas are false because they're old, and then we want to appeal to the "ancient wisdom" handed down through the ages.

Either way, if an idea is true, it is not true because it is new or old. Standing the test of time might lend some credibility to an idea. But, we need to look at what the arguments are and ask ourselves whether or not the arguments still make sense.

By calling an idea old or out of date, we excuse ourselves from having to think about it or be challenged by it. This fallacy is a thought-stopper, which is the opposite of clear, critical thinking. At least bad thinking can be corrected. Even a bad motor can be fixed, but a car with no motor at all can hardly be called a car. Invoking this fallacy is like removing the engine.

It is a great danger to be stuck in the mindset of our own culture and our own age just because of popular appeal. Even reading stuff from other modern cultures won't combat the time problem. Those other cultures are still modern. And in our age of globalization, a lot of the cultures start to look alike.

I have a few quotes along this line from Einstein and others. They say that if all you read is modern stuff, it is like wearing blinders. Every age has its own insanities and its own blind spots. The only way to get out of that is to read and take seriously writing from other ages. We can't read the stuff from the future, so we have to read stuff from the past. The Middle Ages, the Renaissance, the Ancient world. And then that might help get you out of the blind spots of the current age. Sometimes, unfortunately, I think we read stuff from the past, but only to laugh at it. A study of the literature of the past can turn into a study of what psychological and sociological forces led these people to think such ridiculous stuff. As opposed to looking these authors in the face, grappling with the ideas they are presenting, and then asking ourselves if those ideas are true or false and why.

"I think that there are ideas that people thought were true back then and we think are false now. Like people used to think the earth was flat. So, time helps develop ideas. Time helps strengthen an idea and its argument."

And in the case of something like the earth and science, we have better technology than we did before. That allows us to know more. But when it comes to philosophy, there is no special equipment you need to do philosophy. You have reason and human experience. That is what we appeal to.

And, by the way, it is a common mistake to think that everyone in the ancient world and the Middle Ages thought the earth was flat. It is a complete fable that people didn't want Columbus to set sail because they thought he would fall off the edge of the world. Absolutely false. That idea was put into a history book written at the end of the 1800s that is just plain terrible history. But, the book was a best seller and the idea has been passed down ever since, even though scholars know it is wrong. Ancient and Medieval Europe knew very well that the earth was a sphere. For example, how many of you are reading or have read *The Divine Comedy*? Or at least the first part, *The Inferno*?

*No hands go up.*

No one. Darn. Well, that book was written in the 1300s, and the entire book is based on a spherical earth. That was pre-Christopher Columbus. There was an Ancient Greek who calculated the circumference of the earth...without a calculator! For educated people, it was common knowledge that the earth is a sphere. The people who worried about Christopher Columbus weren't worried that he would fall off the edge of the earth, they were worried that he wouldn't have enough supplies to make it all the way around. And they were right. Columbus's estimation of the size of the earth was off.

This is a great example of why it is important to read old books. If you had read *The Divine Comedy*, then you would know how ridiculous the Columbus fable is. But even more than that, we are looking for wisdom. If we get a historical detail like that wrong for lack of reading old books, how much more so when it comes to the big and important ideas like the meaning of life, human nature, morality, the fundamental source and nature of reality?

# 25. Fallacies: Ad Hominem

Alright! Today is going to be pretty quick, and we are continuing our series on logical fallacies. Two weeks ago, we talked about the fallacy of equivocation, which is when someone switches the meaning of a word halfway through the argument. And last week we talked about... um...what did we talk about last week?

"Chronological snobbery."

Right. Thank you. Chronological snobbery, which is when someone tries to say that an idea is false because it's old. Two very common fallacies.

Here is an example of another very common fallacy. Again, it is a ridiculous argument, and I wrote it that way to make the fallacy obvious. Hitler believed in progress. Therefore, we should not seek progress. That's the argument.

"The definition of progress can vary."

True! That's a good point. The meaning of that term might be changing or misunderstood. That is in fact a problem with this argument. And that is a problem in general with this particular term that I think we have discussed before. What is progress? But you are right that the definition of terms is a problem here. What else? There is another problem.

"I don't think that just because a bad person believed in something that we shouldn't believe that, too. We don't like him, but that doesn't mean his belief in progress was wrong."

Right. Just because a bad person believed in something, doesn't mean that thing is wrong or bad in itself. This is the fallacy called ad hominem, which means "to the man" or "to the person." The idea is that you are pointing to the person and then saying, "Therefore it is false." Instead of examining the idea and the arguments for or against the idea, you are looking at a person. That is a fallacy. If an idea is false, it's not because the people who believed it were idiots or were bad people.

On the other side of this coin is also the appeal to authority, another form of ad hominem. The difference is that instead of appealing to how bad or stupid someone is, you try to appeal to someone's intelligence or good character. If an idea is true, it is not true because it is believed by someone who is a genius. Someone might be a genius and a trustworthy authority on one subject and be completely wrong in another. Being great at one subject doesn't somehow mean that all of that person's opinions are true.

This appeal to authority happens often with scientists. Our age in particular seems to worship science and scientists. How many times have you seen a quote from Albert Einstein that has nothing to do with physics? Unfortunately, not all scientists are very good philosophers. As a matter of fact, I have read some books by brilliant scientists that take up philosophical topics, and they are terrible books. They may sell a ton of copies and convince a lot of people, but that doesn't make the arguments and ideas in the books any better. To anyone who knows philosophy, those books are just demonstrations of the ignorance of the author.

For example, Lawrence Krauss, a very good physicist, wrote a book called *A Universe from Nothing*. The entire book is based on the fallacy of equivocation, which we discussed. In the beginning of the book he admits that he doesn't understand the way philosophers define nothing. So then he writes a whole book on it.

*Laughter.*

Then, he makes up his own definition. At one point in the book, he identifies something and says that he is going to call that nothing. If it can be described, then it is not nothing, it is a thing. That is a fallacy and terrible philosophy, and he received a lot of criticism for it. That's just one example.

The expertise and accomplishments of any person in any one particular subject do not make him or her an authority on all other subjects. But that doesn't keep them from making public statements and writing books about all other subjects. Don't get me wrong, some of them have done their homework and know what they are talking about, but the arguments have to be evaluated on their own merit, not accepted simply because they come from a scientist.

Anyway, ideas are not true or false because of who believes them or not. There are cases where someone or a group of people may be a valid authority on a topic. In that case, we can trust them, but their authority has to be established first.

So, happy Philosophy Friday.

# 26. Your Questions

Today we are going to discuss questions that you have. You may even be wondering if your question is a philosophical question.

"What do you mean?"

For example, a common question that people have is "what is the meaning of life."

"How do you judge a person?"

"Are you judging me?"

*Laughter.*

Yeah! Great question. And that certainly is a philosophical question. It has to do primarily with ethics which asks questions about right and wrong, what is good. But to judge a person you also have to know about that person, and how well do we really know anyone? In theory, if you judge a person, you need to know both everything about that person and you have to know the standard by which to judge. It is much easier to judge actions, but even that requires that you know about real right and wrong. And that, again, brings us to the basis of ethics. Why are right and wrong what they are? What makes them right or wrong. If there is no standard, then there is also no judgment.

"Has anything ever been solved by philosophy?"

I like that question! I would say, yes.

There were a lot of things solved. At one time I think there was a beautiful and accurate philosophy that a lot of people believed. Unfortunately, over time, that view just seemed to fall out of fashion. Most people tend to go along more with fashion than with rigorous thinking about truth. When that philosophy fell out of fashion, some others popped up that have since caused a lot of confusion because they contain some flaws in their starting points. Now it looks like philosophy is just a big mess. A lot of people look at philosophy and say, "How can there be any true philosophy? All the philosophers just disagree with each other." That is sad because it can be very beautiful.

One example of a problem that was "solved" by that old forgotten philosophy is science. The scientific method is not a result of science but came from a way of looking at the world and the medieval understanding of nature as harmonious and ordered. Philosophy and science really have a common origin that begins with wonder when looking at the world. In our day, that philosophy is forgotten, so philosophy so-called and science don't always seem to get along.

But what philosophy does is provide a framework for looking at reality and making decisions, even making judgments, like we just talked about. At one time the dominant philosophy said that every human being has dignity and worth and is deserving of medical care, so they invented hospitals. At one time the dominant philosophy saw the dignity of the intellect of every person, and so they started educating everyone, even poor people in the street. The philosophy of an age has an enormous effect on what that age produces, and the same is true for each individual.

"What makes a philosopher good or bad?"

The first important quality is an honest search for truth, that they are a philo-sopher, a lover of truth. They want truth for truth's sake.

The ultimate judge of whether a philosophy is good or not is whether it matches up with reality. Does the philosophy make sense of reality, which is different from explaining away reality? Those are different things.

One of the reasons I think that some philosophers have such strange philosophies is a combination of a lack of being in touch with reality, intelligence, and a certain kind of selfishness. One of my professors used to talk about ideas that are so crazy only someone with a PhD could believe them. The people who survived the holocausts talk about their torturers not as these malicious madmen, but as people who seemed to be indifferent.

It was an academic exercise for them. By separating themselves from the reality of the humans in front of them, really intelligent people are very much in danger of living in their own heads. This really is a danger that smart people face, the ability to perform all sorts of mental gymnastics to justify crazy ideas and somehow avoid reality and things that are obviously true. To rationalize is to tell yourself rational lies. It is too easy for smart people to be very logical and yet completely out of touch with reality. Logic is the thought process. But keeping in humble contact with reality is fundamental for philosophy.

Good philosophy also stays within the bounds of philosophy and uses philosophical tools. You can't paint with a piano, and you can't philosophize using the tools and methods of literary criticism. This is important because it is not uncommon for people to arrive at a scientific conclusion about some properties of the universe and then proclaim that they have figured out the basic nature of reality. Quantitative descriptions of properties of reality are not the same thing as the essence of the thing itself. There is a great temptation today to substitute physics for philosophy, but it is an injustice to both physics and philosophy to do so.

"What do you think about the government listening in to our conversations and monitoring all of our data or withholding certain information from us?"

Interesting question. I am sorry to say I won't answer your question directly and tell you my own thoughts on this, which are not very well formed anyway. But however we answer that question will be based on our philosophy. In particular, what is the purpose and domain of government? What is the basis of government, and does the government have rights? Also, do humans have the right to privacy? How much? More importantly, why? What is the basis of our rights? Why do we have them in the first place? If you can figure out the answers to those questions, then you are on your way to establishing what is really right and what is really wrong in that case. I get the impression most people just go with how they feel or what they want in that case.

"How do you determine whether something is living or if it is inanimate?"

Some people argue that this is biology, but others would argue that this is the philosophy of biology. You have to first come up with the definition of a living thing, and that definition does not come from biology itself, which is the study of living things. It is philosophy that draws that line for biology. It is also philosophy that determines how biology and science are done. The scientific method is not something that science discovered. The scientific method tells us *how* science discovers, and it came from the philosophy of science. Most people would find it surprising that this method actually grew out of Europe in the Middle Ages. Philosophers there recognized that there was a regularity, measure, and order to nature.

To answer your question, though, living things have three characteristics. First of all, there is nutrition. The organism has some way, however crude it may be, of taking in matter from somewhere and incorporating it into its own structure. Second, there is generation, some way of reproducing. Then, something I just read recently which I thought was interesting, living things have heterogeneous composition. In other words, it is made up of different parts and different kinds of matter that all work together to sustain the life of the thing. If you pick up a stone and take a sample from anywhere in the stone, you will find the same composition, the same kind of matter. That is called homogenous composition. But if you do that for a living thing you will get different kinds of matter and different parts of the body.

"So, what does a living thing have that a robot doesn't have?"

Well, a robot doesn't do any of those things naturally. A robot might do those things if we program them to do that, but that is artificial. Generation and nutrition are not natural, organic processes in robots. First of all, we tell it to do that, and secondly, not all robots do all three of those things.

"What if something is living but we define it as non-living?"

That is part of the process. That is why we study things. If we describe something the wrong way, then we want to investigate to find out. Then, we admit we were wrong and reclassify it. But it is important to remember that if there is a wrong way of thinking about something, that implies that there is also a right way of thinking about it.

"Why do we consider nature beautiful?"

Interesting question. I will actually come back to this in my very last lecture, but here is the intro. When we call something beautiful, we are using a term and applying it to something. So, we need to figure out what that term means. What is beauty? Where is beauty? If beauty is only in my mind, then how can I apply it to a symphony or a novel or a mountain landscape or even a mathematical theorem? It is one thing, but it can be applied to all of these very different things. Very interesting, and very important. In my mind, beauty is one of the top two reasons that I teach physics. More to come on that in the last lecture.

"Are there cosmic answers to these questions?"

Yes, because as long as our language and our philosophy can accurately describe reality, then there are answers. There is truth, and something is true if the thought matches the thing itself.

"I sometimes wonder why I take pleasure in the things I like. When I'm eating some food, and I'm really enjoying it, I'm like, why? In a little while it's going to be over, my enjoyment will be over. I enjoy the pizza, and then it's gone."

"It's going to be ok, man."

*Laughter.*

"But it's all just meaningless. Does that make any sense?"

You are on to something. But let's start with this. How do you know it is all meaningless?

"I don't know. I guess I just don't see the meaning."

Right. Here is the interesting thing though: you have the sense of meaning. If there was no meaning, then why would we have a sense about meaning? How would we even have an idea about meaning? The very fact that we look for meaning is an important bit of evidence. If no humans ever had eyes, we would have no concept of light. The very fact that we have eyes is due to light. We only have the capacity for knowing things that exist.

You only have ears because there is such a thing as sound. Your ears might not work, but the very existence of your ears implies that sound exists. So, if we have this capacity for thinking about and wanting meaning, that would seem to imply that there is such a thing as meaning. The next thing, then, is to find it, and to find out the truth about it. Not just making it up for ourselves. What is that thing in reality? If we are just making it up, then we are just playing mind games with ourselves. So, I don't know what the meaning of your pizza is, but focus on the idea of meaning itself. That might get you somewhere.

"Is there life outside of earth?"

Good question. Very interesting. That is a question that philosophy cannot answer. That is a question that is probably not even in the realm of science because there is no way to directly test it. We never know when we might find life right around the next corner. We won't know until we find it. Until then, we just don't know.

The philosophical point is that when it comes to the existence of any one particular thing in our universe, we cannot know for sure that it exists until we meet it. Science can sometimes figure out that something is possible, but whether it is there is a matter of experience.

"Is there a way to figure out if there is heaven or hell or where you will go? How do we know how that works?"

Good question. What differentiates philosophy from religion is that religion will look at a set of Scriptures or a revelation of some kind and use it as the foundation of its ideas. Science takes experimental evidence as the basis, and history takes primary source documents and archeological evidence as its basis. Philosophy asks what we can know just from reason and experience. There have been philosophers who have argued for an afterlife even apart from any religious revelation. I don't know of any philosophers have argued for heaven and hell, in the way we think about them, from a specifically philosophical standpoint, but Plato and Aristotle, for example, maintained that the soul continues to live after the body in some way.

"What is science and how does it work?"

Good question! Very appropriate. Science, in its most basic form, is the habit of investigating and what we know about measurable physical quantities, patterns, and interactions between objects. And we get that information through experiments. That's why a question like "Is there life on other planets" is often regarded as not scientific, because there is no experiment for that.

It's important to realize that science cannot tell us about the nature and existence of the thing, which is what philosophy is really interested in. For example, take this table. Science can tell us a lot about this table and about its measurable physical characteristics. But none of those things tell us about the essence of the table. What is it that *makes* it a table?

That is one of the things that makes quantum physics so difficult. We don't have any direct experience with those things, so we don't know the essence or the "whatness" of the things. What is that thing in itself? All we can get are some of the measurable characteristics. If I told you about the characteristics of a person, eye color, hair color, personality, height, weight, body type, that is very different from meeting the person himself or herself. And you can never meet an electron. You can never have an encounter with an electron, but we can come up with some information about the electron's characteristics.

# 27. Newton's Flaming Laser Sword

For today, I am going to show you five minutes of a YouTube video, and your job is to pick out the bad philosophy in it. This is an interesting video that I found a few years ago, and I know this is a popular channel. But, there is a logical fallacy that is related to something we have discussed somewhere in the first five minutes. Ok. Here we go.

[I play the first five minutes of *Did the Past Really Happen* by Vsauce. Try it. Watch the video and see if you can pick it out.]

What do you think?

"Is it Newton's Flaming Laser Sword?"

Ok. Maybe. What about it? What does it say?

"That if something can't be proven by experiment, then it can't be proven at all."

Close. It says if it cannot be tested by experiment, then it is not worthy of debate. So, what's wrong with that?

"There's no experiment we can do to see if there are aliens or life on other planets, but that is still worthy of debate."

Ok. That's one problem. According to the rule, those things are not worthy of debate, but you might try to make an argument for why those things are worthy of debate. But someone could just point back to the Sword and say, "Nope. No experiment, so not worthy of debate." So, in other words, stop arguing about it because experiment won't settle it.

"So, there's no debate at all because if you can prove it you don't need to debate it."

I think it's saying that the debate consists of doing the experiments to try to falsify the idea.

"It's kind of like putting philosophy and science into one, where they are completely opposite. Science deals with the physical stuff, but philosophy is the complete opposite of that."

I wouldn't call them complete opposites, but you're onto something there. But think about the statement, "If it cannot be tested by experiment, then it is not worthy of debate." Think about that statement for a moment. Now, can *that* statement be tested by experiment?

"No."

"Yes. You can have a debate but not have an experiment that proves it."

Is that an experiment, though? Think about what goes into an experiment. You do experiments in class. You design your own experiments and analyze experiments.

You see, the problem is that it is actually self-refuting. It says that if something cannot be tested by experiment, then it is not worthy of debate. But that very statement cannot be tested by experiment. So, that very statement is not worthy of debate.

One of the problems, though, is that it is very vague. What does it mean to not be worthy of debate? It means that it's neither true nor false. He's saying that the only source of truth is science. Science is the only way to know. We talked about that much earlier in the year, and it is self-refuting. It's actually an irrational belief to believe that science is the only way to know what's true because that is not science. It's a philosophical statement about science. But the statement cuts off philosophy as irrelevant or a matter of pure opinion and preference.

It is really easy to watch a video like that and forget that you're supposed to think critically about what you're watching. Here is how I found this video. I decided to look on YouTube for some interesting, short philosophical video that I could show in philosophy club and then discuss. I had heard about this channel, so I went there and searched for philosophy, and this video came up. I started watching, noticed the fallacy and decided to use it for Philosophy Friday.

But I showed it to a friend to see if she could pick out the fallacy, and we went through the same thing that we just went through. And she commented on how the entertainment and the graphics and the anecdotes are so well done that it would be very, very difficult for anyone to pick out that problem. And it is funny and entertaining and really interesting, and in the middle of it he puts forward this idea as a great philosophical principle, when it is really an irrational idea.

"You should make a video about that."

Maybe I have!

Here is the history of the Sword. There was a scientist who was fed up with philosophers asking tough questions, so he wrote a paper and introduced Newton's Flaming Laser Sword. He didn't realize that he was articulating, in a vague way, an old idea that has been shown to be logically problematic. Isaac Newton had nothing to do with this flaming sword.

So, Happy Philosophy Friday. Be careful about what you watch! This is why we are trying to train you to be better critical thinkers. You have all kinds of ideas thrown at you all the time, but you have to evaluate them with sound reasoning.

# 28. Would You Rather...

Good morning everyone!

Your question this morning is a "would you rather" question. Have you guys ever seen these before?

"Yeah."

There are some really funny ones out there. But today's question is more philosophical. You have the option of being very poor but very wise, and let's say it's some situation where you can't use your wisdom to get money. You are poor and you'll just be poor and wise. And as long as you are poor, you'll be wise. The other option is to be very rich, but very foolish.

"If you're rich can you become poor? Like if someone steals from you?"

No. Let's say that you will just always be rich and foolish if you choose that, and it can't change.

"So, what do we define as wise?"

That is a good question! What is wisdom. Let's say it consists of primarily knowing about the fundamental nature of reality and, therefore, knowing what is really important, knowing what is truly of value. That will also give you an understanding of how to navigate situations and how to make good choices because you know what is truly important because you know about the nature of reality.

And this is different from being merely intelligent. There have been people in history who were very intelligent whom most of us would also describe as foolish. For example, the doctors in the concentration camps who tortured people to find out how much pain people could withstand. Very intelligent, but they set new standards for human torture. Intelligence and wisdom are not necessarily the same thing.

"What would the definition of foolish be?"

Lacking an understanding of the true nature of reality and of what is really important. Therefore, you would also not have a reliable guide for making decisions about your life.

"Why can't you be taught to be wise with all the money you have?"

Wisdom is not necessarily the kind of thing that can be taught. It's not just a collection of information.

"If you're rich then you can go travel the world and learn from experience."

Right, but not everyone learns wisdom from experience. There are ways of going through life and traveling and not becoming any wiser. Some people travel the world and read the great books of the past in order to pass judgment on them rather than learn from them. It all depends on the attitude of the person. Is he having these experiences as a critic or as a student?

Also, if someone is foolish, then he will not have the wisdom to use his money that way. The worst thing about being foolish is that you do not know you are a fool. Only someone who knows that he needs wisdom can begin to seek it. Knowing that you're foolish is a piece of wisdom. One of my quotes on the wall says, "There are two kinds of people in the world: the fools who think they are wise and the wise who know they are fools." Marinate on that for a while.

"If you are so wise, then how did you make decisions that led you to become poor?"

Good question. For this situation, let's just say that the magic genie who set it up has made it that way. That is just the choice you have to make.

I want you to notice an assumption that you are all making, that the wise man would want to be rich. Maybe it is the case that a wise person would choose poverty. There have been a number of people considered to be very wise who chose a life of poverty. Maybe they understand that money is really not that important in the first place. I know a group of people who have made a choice like that.

"They are both content in their own minds. The wise person knows his place and what's important. But the rich person is content with just having a lot of things, and they won't have the capacity to know the difference."

Right. And you used a good word there: content. Even the rich and foolish person is going to be content to some degree and in some sense of the word *content*. But which one is more likely to bring you *real happiness*? Money without wisdom or wisdom without money? If you remember, we talked about real happiness before and whether money can buy it. Is that deep joy the kind of thing that comes from money or wisdom?

Keep in mind here, too, – this is important – that wisdom is not the same thing as knowing a lot of stuff. It's understanding it. For example, imagine a girl who has grown up in the circus and she has known and loved horses her whole life. From before the time she could walk, she was familiar with the feel of a horse's mane and the contours and muscles of the horse's back. She rides horses, she sleeps with them, she cleans them, she plays with them. But then she is put in school and the teacher asks her to define a horse. How can she sum up her love of and experience with horses? She can't answer the question. So the teacher calls on the snotty know-it-all and he rattles off the perfect textbook definition of a horse, but the closest he has ever come to a horse was the time he almost got run over in the street by a horse-drawn cart. Who has more wisdom about horses?

"The girl."

So, it's not a piece of information. Which would you rather be, if given this type of choice, when it comes not just to horses but to reality and existence itself?

I will end with this. Over the last year I have become friends with some friars. I go once a month and spend a day with them. They wear robes, and they have taken a vow of poverty. So, they have voluntarily chosen the poverty of the first option. And the joy that these men exude blows me away. They spend their lives serving the poor in various ways. These are the guys I go to when I am looking for advice.

Ultimately, this is a decision that you need to make. This question turns out to be very real. You are evaluating what real happiness is. Which are you going to pursue with more ardor in your life? It's not necessarily that you have to have one without the other in reality, but where are you going to put your greater effort?

# 29. When Someone Insults You

Your Philosophy Friday question is potentially very relevant to you. We are going to get practical here. Let's imagine someone makes a negative comment about you. I know this never happens to any of you.

*Laughter.*

But let's just imagine for a moment that someone says something bad about you either to a friend, to your face, on social media, or whatever the case might be. What is the best way to react? We can talk about this from a psychological perspective of what emotions arise within you or how you might be able to make that person really angry. But we are concerned right now with figuring out what is the wisest choice.

"Laugh it off."

"That never works."

Works for what? What's the outcome that it doesn't "work" for?

"Revenge."

What does revenge do?

"Makes it even."

"It makes you feel satisfied."

"I just makes it worse."

"I feel like if someone says something bad to you, you have the right to say something bad back to them."

Ok, ok. Calm down. There are some interesting things to talk about here.

First of all, rights. Where do rights come from? We've talked about this before.

Now, let's start thinking about our options here as rationally as we can. Someone makes a negative comment about you. How does that hurt you? What does that do to you?

"No one wants to hear something bad about themselves. Unless maybe it's constructive criticism. But sometimes people say things out of spite to pull you down. But whether they are trying to be helpful or not, no one likes to hear it."

Right. I don't think any of us like it.

Now, whatever they say is either true or false.

"Could it be their opinion?"

Well, let's take an example. Imagine someone says to me, "Mr. D, your forehead is growing." That's either true or false. I either have a growing forehead, i.e. I am going bald, or I am not. We have talked before about how fact vs opinion is a false dichotomy. In the end, every statement is either true or false.

"What about, 'You're ugly.'"

Some of these statements might just be statements about their feelings or they are giving vent to some frustration. What is the content of the statement?

If the statement is true, then you need to ask yourself, is it a bad thing or does it not really matter? Someone says to me, "You're going bald!" Well, that's true. I am going bald. But there's nothing I can do about that. It doesn't really matter. So I just let it go.

If someone says that I'm really mean, then I should probably do something about that. I don't want to be mean, so I will have to work on that somehow. If it is false, then I don't have to worry about it at all. If somebody says something that is not true, then there isn't anything I need to worry about.

When we look at the content of the statement itself, either it's true or it's false. If it's false, then it doesn't matter. If it's true, then I have to decide if it's something I can change and how important it is. It matters or it doesn't matter.

Let's get back to the question about how a negative comment affects you.

"People usually get defensive."

That is how most people react. True. It doesn't necessarily *make* you upset, but you can react that way. There's a difference. Nobody can *make* you do something. They might know your patterns and know how to push your buttons, but *your* reaction is still your reaction that you are responsible for. But what does the statement do to you directly? Somebody makes a negative statement about me. Does that change *who* I am? Does that comment somehow make me a worse person?

My reaction can change me. I can react in a way that makes me a worse version of myself. Do you see the difference? The only person who can affect you is you. It can affect your reputation, but you are not your reputation. Your life does not consist of what other people think about you. You are who you are independent of whatever anyone else thinks or says about you.

The philosophical idea here is to know yourself. Who are you and what are you? And if you can keep that in mind when you are thinking through these situations, then it might change how you react. This is what philosophy is ultimately about: the nature of things in themselves. And then you can think rationally about what the best way to behave is because you have figured out what you are.

# 30. The Apology

Today is going to be story time in Philosophy Friday. I am going to tell you about the beginning of philosophy as we know it today.

It started with this guy Socrates, who lived in Athens in Ancient Greece. He had a friend named Chaerephon. Chaerephon came to Socrates one day and said to him, "I got to go to the Delphic oracle and ask the oracle a question." The Delphic Oracle was kind of like a prophet. She was a mouthpiece of the god Apollo, and whatever the oracle said was regarded as divine and authoritative. People could go and wait a long time, and if they let you in, you could ask the oracle any one question, and the answer was considered the final word on the matter. Oftentimes the answer was in the form of a riddle, but it was taken very seriously.

By the way, do you see the quote on my wall over there that is in Greek? In English it means "Know thyself." I have heard this quote attributed to Socrates, but it was inscribed above the door of the Delphic oracle.

Socrates thought it was great that his friend Chaerephon got to ask a question, because not a lot of people did that. He asked him what question he asked. Chaerephon told him, "I asked the oracle if there was anyone wiser than my friend Socrates." Socrates was upset at this. "Why would you waste your one question? That is a stupid question! Why would you do that? I could have told you the answer to that question because I know that I am not wise."

But Chaerephon asked him if he wanted to hear the oracle's answer. Socrates said he already knew what the oracle would say, because Socrates knew that he was not wise. Chaerephon told him anyway, and he said that the oracle said no one was wiser than Socrates. Socrates took this seriously, and he was puzzled because he was not sure of a lot of things, but he was pretty sure that he was not wise. He thought the oracle had given him a divine mission in the form of a riddle to seek out and find someone wiser than him, and then he would take that person to the oracle and demand the answer to a riddle. He would say, "Look, here is someone wiser than me. Now, what is the answer to the riddle?"

Socrates was sure that it would not be hard to find people wiser than him. He went to the politicians of Athens. These were the men who had taken on themselves the responsibility of governing the people. So, they must have known about the nature of justice, the nature of goodness, what it means to be a human being, and what makes a good community. That is wisdom! Socrates was going to find one of these people and bring him to the oracle and get the answer to the riddle.

The problem was that, as he started asking questions to the politicians about the nature of humanity, justice, goodness, and beauty, he found that they could not answer his questions, or they contradicted themselves. It turned out that they were not really wise after all. Socrates realized they had something in common with him: none of them had this wisdom. But the difference was that Socrates knew that he was not wise. The politicians were not wise, but they thought they were wise. So, was Socrates wiser than the politicians? Yes, but only because he knew he was not wise.

He then moved on to the poets and artists of Greece who were the next most likely people to be wise. The people of Athens loved their plays. They held contests every year, and some of those plays are still around today. You guys have read Oedipus and Antigone?

"Yeah."

Those were written by Sophocles in Athens. Another playwright, Aristophanes, wrote a play in which Socrates is a character.

Anyway, Socrates went to these artists and poets who must have had wisdom because they wrote so beautifully about life and human experience. As he questioned them, he found that they really didn't know what they were talking about. They had a way with words, they had a way of inspiring people, but they themselves didn't have wisdom about the nature of what it means to be a human being or the true good. Again, these people thought that they were wise even though they were not. So, again, Socrates was wiser than them because he was not wise either, but he knew that he was not wise.

Socrates moved on to the craftsmen, the people who make things. They worked with materials and built things, so maybe they knew about the nature of stuff. It turned out they were not wise either. So, Socrates realized that the oracle was right. No one was wiser than Socrates because no one was really wise. But Socrates had the wisdom to know that he was not wise.

Again, I refer to the quote, "There are two kinds of people in the world, the fools who think they are wise, and the wise who know they are fools." You can always tell the first kind because they just want to rule the world, the school, the country, whatever it might be. If only I was in charge and everybody did things my way, then everything would be all right.

So, yay for Socrates and his wisdom. But there was a major problem here. He had now embarrassed almost all of the most powerful people in Athens by exposing their ignorance, and the unruly youths have watched what Socrates did. They could then imitate him and embarrass people just for fun. They started asking people questions, not because they really wanted wisdom, but because they wanted to tear people down and play jokes on them.

There were some people, though, who recognized that Socrates was searching for wisdom about truth, justice, goodness, and beauty. So, they started following him as disciples because they wanted wisdom, too. And that is the true spirit of philosophy. Socrates called himself a philosopher, a lover of wisdom, not because he had wisdom but because he loved it and desired it. That is the basic meaning of the word "amateur," also. It comes from the Latin word for love because the amateur loves the subject, as opposed to the professional who gets paid for it.

Now, because these unruly youths started imitating Socrates, he was brought to court in his old age on charges of corrupting the youth. His defense speech is called the Apology, which means "defense" in Greek, not saying I'm sorry. Plato wrote it, and Plato was there at the trial. Is this a word for word account of what happened at the trial? Probably not, but that wasn't the style of recording speeches in Ancient Greece anyway.

The way the trial worked was that the accusers spoke first in front of the jury, which was about 500 citizens of Athens. Then the accused got to give his defense. Then there was some questioning back and forth, and then the jury gave a decision. Socrates was found guilty. Socrates then got to recommend a punishment. Everyone expected him to recommend exile, and that is probably what they would have done. Just kick him out of Greece. But Socrates thought that he was doing Athens a favor, that he was waking them up from their slumber of foolishness. He recommended that they give him a salary and take care of him for the rest of his days. They elected instead to kill him by giving him hemlock to drink. After he got this decision, he got to give one more speech.

This work, the *Apology*, is one of a handful of things I would make everybody read if I could. You can easily find it for free on the internet; Plato's copyright ran out about 1,500 years ago. I even recorded it and put it on my YouTube channel. We are not going to read the whole thing, but this week and next week we are going to read parts of it.

Here is one lesson I want you to take away. Just as there were people around Socrates who followed him because they wanted to find wisdom and truth and goodness and there were others who imitated him just because they wanted to embarrass people, so there are those same groups of people today. Some people take up philosophy because they have a love of wisdom; they want to know what truth is. But there are others who take up philosophy because they want to use it as a stick to beat ideas they don't like. Unfortunately, I saw a lot of students who had this attitude when I was earning my BA in philosophy. People were just cynical and loved to ridicule ideas. These people are not really doing philosophy, but they are using the methods of philosophy for a selfish end. They give philosophy a bad name. If you have lost that initial sense of wonder and the desire to know, then you are no longer doing philosophy. The question for each of you is, where do you stand? Do you use philosophy, or do you abuse philosophy? Or do you stand back and pass judgment on philosophy, like Socrates' accusers at the trial? You decide.

We are going to read just the beginning here. So, read along with me.

How you have felt, O men of Athens, at hearing the speeches of my accusers, I cannot tell;

Right away, what is he doing? He is admitting ignorance. "I do not know." That is one of the main points. He knows he is not wise, and you see that in the very first line.

Now, turn to the last line. The trial is over, Socrates has been given his sentence, and this is the end of his final word to the citizens of Athens.

The hour of departure has arrived, and we go our ways, I to die and you to live. Which is better, God only knows.

Again, he's talking about this knowledge. Who has knowledge? Certainly, none of us humans. But this god figure, if there is a god, he would have wisdom, because as god he would know everything. Plato wrote his dialogues very carefully, so it is almost certainly intentional that he starts and ends the work this way.

Let's go back to the beginning and see what he says next.

But I know that their persuasive words almost made me forget who I was.

Another very important point. Made me forget who I was. What is inscribed above the door of the Delphic oracle? Know thyself. And here he is saying that he almost forgot who he was. After listening to them he almost doesn't know himself any more. This relates a bit to what we talked about last week when someone says something mean about you. If you listen to them, it is really easy to forget yourself, to forget who and what you are. He refers to their persuasive words. Words can be persuasive. If you are listening to persuasive words without thinking critically about them, it is really easy to be led astray.

"Is that what he is saying, that they are persuasive but it's not true? They are saying he is something, but it is a lie."

Right. And that is the art of rhetoric, to convince people. This is what – not to pick on lawyers, but there are some good lawyer jokes out there and I have some good friends who are lawyers – but that's part of what lawyers do sometimes. Whether it's true or not we don't care. We are just going to argue for our case and try to convince people that it's true. You look for a loophole or something. As opposed to the philosopher who wants to cut through the rhetoric. The philosopher can look at the persuasive words and say, "Yes, but you made these logical mistakes here. It's not really true, even though your speech was very beautiful."

We will come back to this work next week and learn another lesson from it.

# 31. Boxing with Shadows

Today we are going to continue our reading of the *Apology*. There is another part of this that I wanted to talk about with you guys. As a reminder, last week we talked about the story of Socrates and read a little bit from the first paragraph.

The second paragraph is really important, I think, because it gets at a major problem in philosophy. That problem is our preconceived ideas, the things we think we already know. Especially the prejudices we have built up against people or systems of thought.

Follow along with me as we read. Remember that his accusers have just spoken against him, and now it's his turn. And he is going to begin by responding to his very first accusers. Pay attention.

> And first, I have to reply to the older charges and to my first accusers, and then I will go to the later ones. For I have had many accusers, who accused me of old,

This is a little strange. What's he talking about? Many accusers who accused me of old. This is his first time being brought to court. Why is he talking about accusers from of old?

> And their false charges have continued during many years; and I am more afraid of them than of Anytus and his associates, who are dangerous, too, in their own way.

Anytus and his associates are the guys who are there in court accusing him. But he is saying these other people, whoever they are, he is more afraid of them than of the people in court speaking against him.

> But far more dangerous are these, who began when you were children, and took possession of your minds with their falsehoods, telling of one Socrates, a wise man, who speculated about the heaven above, and searched into the earth beneath, and made the worse appear the better cause.

This phrase, "making the worse appear the better cause," means taking something bad and making it look good. This is just convincing people. This is rhetoric. This is advertising! People trying to convince you that you need things you don't really need. And it was an expression of a bad thing.

So, what's he talking about, the people who began when you were children?

> These are the accusers whom I dread; for they are the circulators of this rumor, and their hearers are too apt to fancy that speculators of this sort do not believe in the gods. And they are many, and their charges against me are of ancient date, and they made them in days when you were impressible - in childhood, or perhaps in youth - and the cause when heard went by default, for there was none to answer.

So, what's he saying? He's talking about people just saying things. People in the marketplace talking. Rumors going around about this guy Socrates, and all these men who are sitting in the jury heard all this stuff. And what happened? They built up these impressions as they heard all this stuff about this guy Socrates who goes around, but they are all just rumors. Those prejudices that have built up are the hardest things to overcome.

So, in your search for truth, in your pursuit of wisdom, the hardest thing to get past are your own biases and prejudices. Those are the things that are just absorbed. One of the reasons they are so hard to get past is because they are not presented clearly and explicitly. They are attitudes that we pick up from society. They are the things that we just assume, and they are the hardest things to see because they are our assumptions. It's as if they are the lenses through which we see everything else. We don't see them, but we see everything else by them.

One example of this is the fable that everyone thought the earth was flat and Columbus proved them wrong. We've talked about this before. You can't remember who told you because you picked it up from multiple places and it's just part of what we all think we know. The same is true of the biases and prejudices you've built up over the years, and you don't even realize that they are there.

Even when we learn the truth about the story of Columbus, that is only one piece of the puzzle. There remains the impression that we have of the people of that time. Closed-minded, dogmatic, prideful, defensive, and against any type of progress or change. That is what we think of the people of the Middle Ages as a result of fables like the Columbus story, and that bias doesn't automatically get corrected once we know the truth about Columbus. It's that kind of thing he is talking about here.

> And, hardest of all, their names I do not know and cannot tell; unless in the chance of a comic poet.

Here he is talking about Aristophanes who put Socrates into his play *The Clouds*. That is probably the one case where he can say, "Look, this is who said it and this is exactly what he said." The rest is vague and fuzzy.

> But the main body of these slanderers who from envy and malice have wrought upon you - and there are some of them who are convinced themselves, and impart their convictions to others - all these, I say, are most difficult to deal with; for I cannot have them up here, and examine them, and therefore I must simply fight with shadows in my own defense, and examine when there is no one who answers.

The problem is that he can't bring these accusers into court and say, "You said this. Can you back this up with evidence?" There is no clear objection, just an attitude. If it is a clear objection that can be stated, then he can answer, but that is not what happened. It's just this vague crowd of people from their past, where they've built up these ideas. It's very hard to get over, because often times it is the things that we know most certainly that we really don't know.

I will ask you then to assume with me, as I was saying, that my opponents are of two kinds - one recent, the other ancient; and I hope that you will see the propriety of my answering the latter first, for these accusations you heard long before the others, and much oftener.

Trying to come to philosophy to examine ideas with an unbiased mind is extremely difficult. That doesn't mean we take everything and throw it out the window. But when we look at a set of ideas, instead of reacting to it, we examine it rationally and look at the evidence. Not easy, but necessary to learn to think this way.

This probably happens nowhere more often than in politics and with hot-button social issues. We just have these gut reactions. People react, get emotional, get angry. We are emotional creatures, and our emotions are important, but our emotions are not the best way to form an opinion.

# 32. No More Human Interaction

Your question for today is this. Imagine that you are offered a deal. I got this from *The Book of Questions*, by Gregory Stock. I have gotten some other questions from there, too. Anyway, you can have everything you would ever want materially. The hitch is that you can never interact directly with another human being again. Even if you were to see someone on the other side of a glass, you are still seeing them directly.

"How would you interact with people, then?"

You can still communicate through phone or chat because you are hearing or seeing each other through some technology, but you can never interact directly with another human being again. You just can't have direct contact through one of your five senses. But you can have anything else you want. House, car, movie theater in your house, food, technology...you name it. Everything you want just all gets delivered by drones or robots or something. Would you take that deal? Why or why not?

"What if you need surgery?"

Robotic surgery.

"I wouldn't take it. If you can't interact with anyone, then that means you can't interact with your family, your friends. Who would choose material things that will only give you short term satisfaction in place of being able to be physical with your loved ones?"

"I think you would go crazy. With no one else to talk to, you start talking to yourself. That's not good."

Crazy is not good?

"Even if you had all that stuff and could do whatever you want, it wouldn't be fun because you wouldn't have anyone to do it with. If you have stuff, you want to share it with people."

"What if you had kids?"

Well, there are ways of having children today without having direct human contact.

"How?"

Well, you couldn't be a mother, at least not the natural way through pregnancy, because then you would have very close contact with your baby. You would have another human being growing inside of you. That's pretty direct. You could have your eggs extracted by robotic surgery and then have children, in a way, by that method. If you are a man, you could send off the necessary materials to fertilize remotely, as crazy as that sounds.

"That's why I wouldn't take that deal."

*Laughter.*

Well, that is something important to consider. That is part of our nature, and an important one, too. That is part of who we are. As philosophers we want to make sure we are considering all the data and taking everything into account.

There is a psychological aspect to this question. The reason I am asking this question for philosophy Friday is that it has to do with the nature of the human being. Again, "Know thyself." Some philosophers have said that man is by nature a social animal. When we look at nature, we see that some animals need a social group to live and thrive. Wolves, bees and ants are social by their nature. Some animals are not. Some animals are independent by their nature.

So, the question is where do humans fall? Are we social by nature so that we need other humans to live and thrive, or are we better off by ourselves? Some philosophers have said man is social by nature, that it is somehow part of us that we ought to exist in a society. Some have said that, no, man is not social by nature, but we have formed social groups because it is better than trying to hack out our own existence in the wilderness.

A lot of your answers were indicating that humans are social by nature. Even with the prospect of all your material wants and needs being met, you still would give that up so you could interact with other humans. You were mostly appealing to the emotional considerations because I said all your physical needs would be met. But if you really were on your own, you would realize how much you need other humans even for survival. It is very difficult for one human to provide for all of his or her own physical needs, let alone all of the emotional needs: human interaction, human touch, family, friends.

There is a topic in philosophy called philosophical anthropology. Anthropology is the study of man. Usually it's the study of human origins. But philosophical anthropology asks about the nature of the human being. Do we have souls or not? Are humans social? These are important questions in philosophical anthropology.

From there, if you know man is by nature social, you can build a whole system of ethics. Everything in philosophy is intertwined. Ethics, what is right and wrong, all comes from what it means to be a human being. If we do something that contradicts our nature as social beings, then we are damaging our own selves.

# 33. Is there Anything so Bad You Could Never Forgive It?

Happy Philosophy Friday! Here is your question for today: is there anything so horrible that you could never forgive?

"If someone murdered my family."

"I think I could never forgive someone who does a school shooting."

"If someone killed me, I don't think I could forgive that."

"Of course, you couldn't, you'd be dead."

*Laughter*

"Yeah, I know. I'm just saying. I don't think I could forgive that."

The idea of forgiving someone who kills you, or tries to, is not totally crazy. Jesus forgave as he was dying on the cross, and Pope John Paul II forgave the man who attempted to assassinate him.

"I would never forgive someone if they killed my dog."

*Laughter*

"No, I'm serious."

It's not uncommon for people to talk about their pets like that. Some people are strongly connected to their dogs and cats.

There are two philosophical points to make here.

First of all, there is the topic of ethics. It is very common for people in our society to say that there are no moral standards, everything is relative or a matter of opinion, but when it comes to some of these things that they could never forgive, they are pretty adamant about some things being objectively wrong. It is important in philosophy to be consistent, that your philosophy at one time of the day matches up with your philosophy at another time of day. We are all philosophers. Everyone has a philosophy about morality. Some people have two philosophies about morality. The goal is to have one, well thought out philosophy. Someone who says at one moment that everything is relative and then says he could never forgive murder is trying to hold two different philosophies at the same time. The whole idea of forgiveness assumes objective morality. If nothing is really wrong, then there is nothing to forgive or not forgive, because no one ever does anything really wrong.

The other point to make here is about human nature. What is the nature of the human being? Are we such that it is better for us to forgive or to hold a grudge? Which one is more in accord with what it means to be a human being?

"I think according to nature we shouldn't forgive because in nature we see animals not forgiving. If you do something wrong to an animal, it won't forgive. It will always react or avoid you."

You bring up a good point here. I think that other animals are reacting according to instinct, whether learned or genetic. Humans, on the other hand, can reflect on the action and make a conscious choice to forgive.

"What is forgiveness? What does that mean?"

Good question. Let's say that it is the conscious choice to not hold an action against someone. They may have done something wrong, but you do not hold that action up between you and that person. That doesn't mean that you forget. That doesn't mean that you put up with abuse. Someone in an abusive relationship can forgive, but he or she should still get out. And sometimes forgiveness is not a one-time thing. The old feelings of resentment can come up again, and the choice has to be made again.

So, I realize that the idea presented to you on movie screens, in the media, and in society in general is not to forgive. We want justice. We cheer when someone gets what's coming to him. But I want to offer a couple of stories that are the opposite of the normal, popular idea. In philosophy we want to challenge our accepted ways of thinking.

Someone mentioned before that she could never forgive a school shooting. Well, some years ago there was a school shooting in an Amish community. A guy walked into one of these small schoolhouses they have, killed a bunch of kids, killed the teacher, and then shot himself. The Amish community came out right away and said that they forgave the man who did this. And as evidence of this, they took all the money that came into their community from people who wanted to express their support and, since they do not accept monetary donations as a matter of principle, they gave it to the family of the man who had done the shooting.

*Shock*

Here is another story. Are you guys familiar with the Rwandan genocide that took place in the 90's?

*Nods*

"Yes. We learn about it in history class."

Ok. Good. There was a woman who survived that genocide, and she wrote a book about her ordeal. Her name is Immaculee Ilibagiza, and the book is *Left to Tell*. Her family was well educated, which was not necessarily common, and well respected in the community. Her father was a school principal. When things started to happen, her father went to the leaders of the community to try to work things out. She never saw him again. Her family scattered, and she found refuge in the home of someone from the other tribe who hid her, along with seven other women in a small bathroom. They placed a large piece of furniture in front of the door so no one would find them if they came in to inspect the house. She lived there for three months. The owner brought them scraps of food to live on. During that time, they could hear what was going on outside since the bathroom had a small window. Brace yourselves, because this is going to be hard to hear. They could hear people being murdered outside. Once, they heard a woman and her baby who were attacked. They killed the woman, but they didn't bother to kill the baby. They knew what would happen. The dogs came and ate the baby.

*Groans*

She eventually got to safety and began to hear the stories about some of her family members. Her brother was killed by a family friend who walked up to him, among a crowd of others, and said that he wanted to see what the brain of someone with a master's degree looked like, and he cut his head open with a machete. When people came in from the outside and placed some of these murderers in prison, Immaculee was given the chance to confront some of her family's murderers. And she forgave them.

"Why?"

Good question. Some of the jailers were angry with her and had the same question. They told her that this was her chance to get back at them, but she said she had to forgive, otherwise the hate would eat her up inside and destroy her. It is not an uncommon story, and I have even heard of friendships growing between people and their family's murderers.

Again, I realize that this is very contrary to the way we normally think about revenge and forgiveness, but I think it is important to hear about real life situations that challenge us and force us to really evaluate our built-in thought patterns.

# 34. What is Wrong with the World?

Today we are going to discuss this question. What is wrong with the world?

"Physics!"

*Laughter.*

Physics is wrong with the world?

"Everything. Everything is wrong with the world."

"People."

People are wrong with the world?

"Bad people."

"Pollution. The Ozone layer."

"Crime."

*Some students are talking in the back.*

People talking when they're supposed to be listening.

*Laughter*

This question was once asked to a group of writers and journalists in England, I think around the year 1900. One of my favorite authors, G.K. Chesterton, gave the shortest response, and I agree with him.

*I write on the board:*

*Dear sirs,*
*I am.*
*Sincerely, G.K. Chesterton*

Why would he write this response? He stopped pointing fingers at everyone else at looked at himself. People are wrong with the world? I'm a people.

*Laughter.*

Crime? I have done things that are illegal. Pollution? I have contributed to pollution. Everything that I can find wrong with the world, I also find in myself.

One important thing to notice about this question is that it implies that there is a way the world *ought* to be. There can't be things wrong with the world if the world wasn't supposed to be some other way. In philosophy, we want to ask, how was the world *supposed* to be? What is *right* for the world?

Another point that this question and Chesterton's answer bring up is that there are two ways of pursuing happiness. One way is by trying to control reality and change my surroundings to the way that I want them to be. I have to try to manipulate everything around me to conform it to my desires and emotions. From this perspective, everything else is wrong, and all of those things have to change in order for me to be happy. The other way to pursue happiness is to conform myself to reality. As long as I am not in harmony with reality and the way things are, I will be discontent. From that perspective, I am the thing that needs to be changed in order for me to be happy.

So, that's it. Happy Philosophy Friday.

# 35. What Would You Do Differently?

You are at the end of your junior year, so you have completed three years of high school.

"Whoa!"

I know. It's crazy, right? If you could go back and do it again, repeat those first three years, what would you do differently?

"Is this philosophical?"

Yes. Good question. I'll explain why this is a philosophical question later. Trust me.

"I would try harder."

"I would start hanging out with some people earlier."

"I don't think I would change anything."

"My grades."

You would change your grades?

"Yeah."

How do you change your grades?

"I would try harder. Like, I tried. I just could have tried harder."

"There was this guy. It was him and his brother, and they didn't get along with a lot of people. So, I started hanging out with his brother, but not him. And now, he's really different."

"I am really different from the way I was Freshman year."

"Me, too."

What do you think has the biggest impact on how you change?

*Almost unanimous:* "Friends."

What do you think is the most important and valuable part of going to school?

"The social aspect."

"Friends."

Well, you still have one year left. You can still make those changes.

"Ugh. It's just one year, though."

True, but if the changes were worth making then, then they are worth making now. If it really is better to live that different way, then it is never too late to start living that way.

In philosophy, we want to know what is the best way to live, and this is based on what is really valuable. We want to intentionally think about what we do so we can conscious decisions about our actions. Otherwise, we are just living day to day without knowing if life could be better. Socrates said that the unexamined life is not worth living. That doesn't mean to stop living, it means to start examining life.

For myself, if I could repeat my high school days, I would reach out more to the kids who weren't so popular. I was popular, I guess. I was a good student. I was co-captain of the football team and track team. I was in the school plays. I got along with everyone. But I stopped hanging out with some kids that I used to hang out with in elementary school. I didn't bully them or anything, but I didn't pay attention to them either. I would hang out with them more if I could do it again.

# 36. What is the Best way to Spend Free Time and Money?

You are on the verge of summer. You have time, money, and, now, a car. Many of you got your driver's licenses this year, and your parents bought you a car, so you have a freedom you haven't had before. How do you spend your time with all this freedom you now have?

"Shopping! Going to the mall and buying stuff."

"Football and working."

You guys spend a lot of time practicing and working out.

"Yeah, I am really not going to have a lot of time."

Well, what will you do when you *do* have some free time? How do you spend your free time now?

"Go to the beach!"

"I spend time with my grandpa."

"My grandma lives down the street, and she says that I haven't come to see her in a while if it's been a few days. So, I go over to her house."

That's good. Anybody else?

"Waterparks."

How often to you think intentionally about how to best use your free time instead of just going with the flow?

"Summer is a time for just going with the flow."

Well, if there are things that are worth your time, then they are worth your time all the time. So, what is the best way to use our time? As philosophers, we want to be intentional about spending our time in the ways that help us reach our full potential instead of just being carried along by what everyone else is doing or expects us to do. Our free time is the best place for us to really invest in becoming our best possible selves. School, work, sports; that time is set for you. But your free time is when you get to engage in the activities that will help you realize your full potential, whatever that may be. And it's probably not just mere entertainment. If nothing else, you want to find ways of being entertained that don't make you dumber. Most entertainment out there probably just makes you stupider. But it's up to you how you spend your time.

For what it's worth, I want to offer a perspective that is probably quite different from what you have heard before. We want to consider all the possibilities, so here is something to consider. There was a young man who lived in Italy in the 1930s named Pierre Giorgio Frassati. His parents were wealthy; they owned one of the leading newspapers in their city. Pierre was a popular, athletic kid. He was a champion skier, he loved to play jokes with his friends, and he studied engineering in college. But he used his free time to serve the poor in his city. He would go around and buy food for the hungry and homeless and play with the kids of those families. He helped people who were sick get the medicine they needed and stay on schedule with it. When his parents bought him a car, which was a bigger deal at that time than it is now because fewer people had cars, he sold the car and used the money to buy a bicycle and food for the poor people.

Unfortunately, he contracted a disease from one of the people he was helping, and he died in his young twenties. But we are all going to die at some point, and some of you may even die young. I had friends in college who died doing stupid stuff. One was drunk and went canoeing in a stream during a heavy rainstorm and drowned. We all die. Are you going to spend your time doing stupid stuff or good stuff? Be intentional about how you spend your time.

# 37. Beauty and Physics – The Final Lecture

*This is the lecture that I give on the last day of class. As I mentioned in the introduction, I substitute a whole class length "freakin' awesome physics Friday" on the days before a long break. This lecture is the culmination.*

Welcome to your last day of physics class! As you already know, today is the final lecture on beauty and physics. Really, it is a synthesis of philosophy and physics. So, it is a combination of Philosophy Friday and freakin' awesome physics Friday. I hope you enjoy it. You can sit back and relax. There will be no test or quiz on any of this stuff. Feel free to stop me and ask questions along the way.

If you can remember back to the first day of class, I asked you why you should take physics. A lot of you gave answers that had to do with the fact that this is a required course, because you needed a good grade, because you want to get into a good college, and so on. Then, if you remember, I told you that one of my primary reasons for teaching physics is that I wanted you to see the beauty in physics. I have tried to point out this beauty along the way. Today we are going to talk about what beauty is, and that will hopefully make more sense out of what I have been talking about all year.

First of all, to give credit where credit is due, I was inspired by and got some of the structure of this talk from an article on beauty and physics by the physicist George Stanciu, who I will quote later on.

Ok. Here we go.

There used to be a show on TV called *Young People's Concerts*, one of the few shows on TV that won't make you dumber. It was led by the famous composer and conductor of the New York Philharmonic, Leonard Bernstein. In one episode, Bernstein conducts the orchestra through a whole movement of one of Mozart's symphonies, and at the end of it he turns to the audience and says something really surprising: "Whether you liked that or not, that was beautiful." For us modern people, there really isn't such a thing as beauty in the first place. Beauty is in the eye of the beholder, so there is no real, objective beauty. If beauty means anything, it means *only* what we like, what we find pleasing. So it makes no sense to us to hear that something is beautiful whether we like it or not.

But Bernstein had already explained in that episode that there is a difference between *taste* and *beauty*. *Taste* is what we are used to, and therefore what we like. If we go to a concert of a band that we like, we are familiar with that music, we know it, we are used to it, so we have a taste for it and really enjoy it.

*Beauty*, on the other hand, may not be recognizable to everyone. The fact is that it takes time to see and understand real beauty in the way that philosophers talk about it. Think about it this way. Some things get better the more you learn about them. Some things get worse. The more I learn about fast food, the worse it gets. Not that it keeps me from getting fast food from time to time. But there are some things that only get better the more I learn about them. Here are some examples from my own experience or from the experience of trusted friends.

First of all, when it comes to wine, I know just a little more than nothing, and I couldn't tell the difference between a ten-dollar bottle of wine and a five-hundred-dollar bottle of wine. But I have friends who have a completely different experience from me when they drink wine, and they can appreciate and recognize a really good wine. That took time, though. Same thing with gourmet food. I can't tell the difference, but I have had some friends who were chefs, and they could pick out all kinds of things going on in a great dish of food, things of which

I am completely ignorant. But it is a better experience for them. They see a beauty I miss out on.

I recently watched a course on classical music that changed the way I listen to music. I will quote from these lectures today. I knew very little about classical music before, and I still don't really know a whole lot, but even what I have learned has changed me. In fact, I remember hearing a famous organ piece by Bach before I watched the lectures, and I remember not getting anything out of it. After the course I heard the same piece, and it was a different experience. I still wouldn't say I had a "taste" for it – I wouldn't necessarily choose to listen to it all the time – but I could hear the beauty in it anyway. I had learned to listen for certain things, and it wasn't the same for me anymore.

Physics and math are also things that have gotten a lot better for me the more I learned about them. It takes some time, especially in mathematics, to move past some of the basics, but once you do, there is so much beauty there. We will get into more of this soon.

I have had a similar experience with looking at the night sky and astronomy. People have asked me if it takes away from the beauty of the night sky because I know about physics and astrophysics and that sort of thing. The answer is absolutely not. Just the opposite! Gazing at the night sky and looking through a telescope gets more exciting the more I know about what I am seeing. It's amazing.

So, the point here is that there is beauty in some things, but it takes time to see it. These are the things that get better the more you learn about them, and these are the tastes that are worth acquiring even though it takes work. Just because we don't see the beauty, it doesn't mean it's not there. Beauty and taste are not necessarily the same thing.

In the course on classical music, the professor, Robert Greenberg, gives a great example from baseball of how knowing the game makes all the difference in recognizing beauty. Imagine that you go to a baseball game with someone who has never seen baseball before. During one of the innings, maybe a team is down by one run. There is one out and a runner on first. The batter hits a groundball to the short stop who snatches up the ball and tosses it to the second baseman who tags the base and throws it to first. A double play! The crowd goes wild! Your friend who does not know about baseball can appreciate something. He can appreciate the athleticism of the players. But he misses the real beauty of the play because he doesn't know the context. Greenberg says, "We can only appreciate that detail if we first understand the large-scale context, the rules of the game, the form of the piece."

So, again, beauty is not always easy to see. It takes work sometimes before you can see beauty.

Now I am going to show you a video clip from a course at Yale University. You may already know that a lot of universities, and even top universities like Yale and MIT, have recorded some of their courses and made them available on iTunes and YouTube and other platforms. This clip is from a course entitled *Frontiers and Controversies in Modern Astrophysics*, and it is a science course for non-science majors. So, don't worry; it's not so far out and difficult that it's impossible for non-physicists to understand. The Professor is Charles Bailyn, one of the leading experts on black holes.

He is going to tell a story about an experience of beauty that he had in a graduate level physics class and the work it took to be able to see it. Keep in mind here that I am trying to build a case by referring to physics, music, and philosophy for the kind of beauty I am talking about. Just before this clip begins, he is talking about an idea in special relativity and how it relates to a bunch of other ideas. Then, he says that the way one idea spawns a bunch of other, unexpected ideas is the kind of thing that makes physicists call a piece of mathematics beautiful. To illustrate this, he tells a story about being in a graduate astrophysics class. Here it is.

I have this vivid memory in graduate school, sitting in a class, you know, the professor was doing the thing that professors do: he was writing down all kinds of miscellaneous information really, really fast from relativity theory and nuclear physics and all sorts of stuff was going up on the board. I was doing the thing that students do where you desperately try and write it all down so that you can then go back and figure out what the hell he was taking about later. And suddenly, in the midst of this rather typical class, I realized what was happening, that in about twenty minutes he was going to put all this stuff together and prove Chandrasekhar's limit. ... And I suddenly saw where all this was going and I sort of wrote down in my notebook "Chandra," underlined it, put my pencil down, and then I just watched for twenty minutes. It was great! It was...the only thing I can compare it to is listening to a great piece of music because it kind of unfolds in time and you see where it's going, and it's just a great feeling. So, don't be condescending to the physics majors when they are working like hell on those problem sets late on a Thursday night because they have access to realms of aesthetic experience that you can only imagine. [laughter] ... It's true, it's true, I promise. But you have to work hard to get there and ask questions.

Notice what he says at the end. It takes work, but there is beauty that is inaccessible otherwise. He also said that it was like a piece of music that unfolds in time. I think that is a great expression: "unfolds in time" like a piece of music. So, I thought I might try something out. The beauty that physicists see in physics is like a great piece of music; so let's listen to a great piece of music to see what it was like for Professor Bailyn. I have picked out a piece of music that has struck me as particularly beautiful, and it comes from a composer who is regarded as one of the greats: Johann Sebastian Bach. This is a piece that is also relatively simple; it is only one instrument. So, there are not a lot of different parts and harmonies to try to listen for. If you are not familiar with classical music, like I am, I recommend just trying to hear each note. It is easy to drift off, so try to pay attention to each note.

*At this point in the lecture I play the Prelude of Bach's First Cello Suite. Alas, dear reader, I do not have a way of playing that piece for you from this book, but you can easily find a recording of it online.*

That is what physics can be like for physicists and what mathematics can be like for mathematicians. Amazing, right? Strange, though, too. I realize most people would call math and physics anything but beautiful, but that is only because they have not developed the eyes that can see it and they are still thinking about beauty as what appeals to them.

Ok, let's get to some specifics. Obviously, I am talking about something other than taste. What, then, is beauty? What are the characteristics?

Here is a quote from Albert Einstein. He said that "a theory is the more impressive the greater the simplicity of its premises is..." keep this aspect in mind. Simplicity will come up again and again here. "...the more different kinds of things it relates..." This has to do with the second aspect of beauty: harmony or balance. "...and the more extended is its area of applicability." That last phrase has to do with the third aspect of beauty, the hardest to describe. Let's go through each of these three characteristics of real beauty.

The first characteristic of beauty is simplicity. Werner Heisenberg, one of the founders of modern physics, referred to this as "frightening simplicity and wholeness." He called it frightening! It is surprising how everything ties together and how much can come out of one idea. Other names for this are one-ness and unity. The main idea here is that disconnected parts do not form beauty. The thing or idea, whatever it is, has to cohere, hold together, be united in some way. Great novels may have a bunch of different smaller stories in them, but something unites them and ties them together in some way.

The second characteristic of beauty has to do with the way the different parts are related to one another. This is called harmony or balance. Heisenberg called this the "proper conformity of the parts to one another and to the whole." Unity implies that everything ties together, but harmony has to do with *how* they are tied together. There must be balance. If a piece of music with a lot of parts is dominated by the harmonies to the point where the melody is obscured, then it is not beautiful. In physics, the various principles should organically flow from and into one another. John Wheeler, a PhD advisor to many great physicists, the co-author of the standard textbook on general relativity, and the guy who coined the name "black hole," said, "Every law of physics goes back to some symmetry of nature." Symmetry is another way of expressing balance and harmony, and it is a characteristic of nature itself.

The third characteristic is the one that I find the hardest to describe. Some names for it are clarity, brilliance, and recognition. In other words, it allows for some insight. It makes sense of things. This is the aspect of beauty that makes us step back and say, "Of course, that's how it had to be." I think we experience this as something like recognition. Have you ever been in a crowded place like a mall and then suddenly seen someone you knew? Seeing a familiar face in a crowd of people you don't know has an aesthetic quality to it. It is the same thing when you get a joke. Someone is telling it, and you are not really getting it. You can't see how it is going to end or what the punch line is going to be, but when you hear it, you know it had to be that way. The whole thing suddenly makes sense. A beautiful law of physics is like the punch line of a joke; it suddenly makes sense of the confusion that came before. And like Einstein said, it is more beautiful the more different things is applies to.

In more than one case, I have heard people refer to "innate inevitability," another way of describing this third aspect of beauty. There is a sense that it had to be that way. I have heard physicists say that when they encountered Einstein's theory of general relativity, they had a sense that is must have been that way. I heard an artist once saying that he got his inspiration from the innate inevitability of landscapes and human physiology. I have had a similar experience looking at landscapes. I don't think I could have planned it or laid it out that way, but I get the strong sense that it just had to be that way. One of the summers I was in college, I was in a country in Central Asia with a group of other college students. At the end of the trip we were debriefing at an empty ski resort at the edge of a mountain range. One day, a few of us pointed to the top of a nearby mountain, and we said, "Let's go!" I don't know how many hours it took to get to the top, but it was awesome! We were on a snow-capped mountain in the middle of July looking out at a whole range of snow-capped mountain after snow-capped mountain. I never, ever could have imagined something like what I saw that day, but I somehow knew it had to be that way.

That innate inevitability is what Leonard Bernstein said made Beethoven's music particularly beautiful. He said that many other composers were much better at technique, cleverness, writing melodies, and making use of the various styles, but all of those skills were "mere dust – nothing compared to the magic ingredient sought by them all: *the inexplicable ability to know what the next note has to be.* Beethoven had this gift in a degree that leaves them all panting in the rear guard. When he really *did* it – as in the Funeral March of the *Eroica* – he produced an entity that always seems to me to have been previously written in Heaven, and then merely dictated to him...predetermined and perfect."

In science, the theories and laws are an important part, but experiments are one of the things that distinguishes science from the other disciplines. Beauty exists even in experiments. The historian of science George Johnson wrote a book called *The Ten Most Beautiful Experiments*, which I recommend. Notice that beauty is part of the title! In the introduction he explains why he chose those particular experiments: "These experiments were designed and conducted with such a straightforward elegance that they deserve to be called beautiful." Elegance and beauty! In experiments! "This is the beauty in the classical sense...." Notice that he clarifies the type of beauty he is talking about: not mere taste. He is talking about this classical, objective sense of beauty. "...the logical simplicity of the apparatus...." See? Simplicity! That's the first aspect of beauty we talked about. "...like the logical simplicity of the analysis, seems as pure and inevitable...." Inevitability, just as in the music of Beethoven and landscapes! "...as the lines of a

Greek statue. Confusion and ambiguity are momentarily swept aside and something new about nature leaps into view."

Again, beauty as I am discussing it here, is not the same thing as taste. Taste is what you like and is conditioned by what you are used to. Beauty is objective and determined by simplicity, harmony, and brilliance, as you can see, I have pulled together from several different disciplines. These are the common factors whether we are talking about music, art, literature, physics, experiments, or mathematics. This beauty really is there, but we often need people to point it out to us.

In our class, I tried to point this out when I showed you that Newton's second law and the equation for impulse and change in momentum are actually the same thing. Newton's laws and the laws regarding momentum are not separate things; there is a unity to them.

Also, Newton's theory of universal gravitation. Up until Newton, people thought that whatever rules governed the movement of the heavenly bodies were different from the rules that governed phenomena on Earth. But Newton tied it all together. He wondered if the force that pulled an apple to the ground and the force that held the moon in orbit around the earth were actually the same. He united them, and then his rule could be applied to every other known body in the solar system. Simplicity and brilliance. One little idea that made sense of centuries of astronomical data and observations of falling bodies and projectiles. That is why I have the equation for the law of universal gravitation on my wall among my quotes. It is beautiful.

At this point I am going to share with you some experiences that people have had of beauty in physics and math in particular. Realize that this type of objective beauty probably exists in many, many different fields of interest, but these are the stories I have found that are relevant to my teaching.

First of all, George Stanciu is a physicist from whom I got some of the structure and material for this talk. He talks about an experience of beauty that he had in geometry. "In the tenth grade, I was forever changed...." Forever changed! By what? A

crush on a beautiful classmate? A first kiss? "...by Euclid's proof
that the prime numbers are infinite...." Probably not the kind of
thing most people would be so affected by. Changed forever by
a mathematical proof! "...an exquisite proof...." So, you all have
taken geometry by now, and so you have done proofs, probably
lots of them. Imagine calling them exquisite! But let's see why.
"...that surprisingly showed in six lines of text an eternal truth."
First of all, it was surprising. That is like the third aspect of
beauty. And in only six lines of text. Simplicity! And, it proved
something that is always true no matter what anyone thinks
about it. Eternal truth in a surprising and simple way. But why
did it change him? "Until that point in my life, I thought truth
did not exist; everything about me changed, the seasons, my
body, and people." Sounds like adolescence. Sound familiar?
"My experience of the human world was that everything was in
flux, sometimes bordering on the absurd. Suddenly,
mathematics presented me with one thing that was unchanging,
a timeless truth, demonstrated in an exceedingly beautiful way;
the 2,500 years between Euclid and me were of no
consequence."

Stanciu then says that his experience of beauty in Euclid was
not unique. He quotes from Bertrand Russell, a famous
mathematician and philosopher. Russell describes his first
encounter with Euclid's geometry as "one of the great events of
my life, as dazzling as first love." As dazzling as first love?! He's
talking about math! What a nerd, right? He probably wore a
pocket protector! [The reader should know that I wear a pocket
protector, so this line usually gets a good laugh.] It gets better.
"I had not imagined there was anything so delicious in the
world." Delicious?! Unfortunately, I think the vast majority of
the human population would drive you to the insane asylum if
you called mathematics "delicious." But that's what it is!

As for myself, I was able to catch a glimpse of this when I
took geometry in high school. I didn't recognize it at the time,
but having read about these other experiences people have had,
and having learned about beauty, I now see what it was. I used
to love looking at some new theorem that needed to be proved,

thinking through what we already knew, and then just kind of seeing in my mind how to get there. Then it was a matter of writing the whole thing out, and it brought this great sense of satisfaction. It made perfect sense. The whole picture just sort of came together.

Again, George Stanciu tells a story about another encounter with beauty in physics. He was taking a class in theoretical physics during the summer, and the class met at seven in the evening. The professor came in a little tipsy one night and announced, "Tonight, gentlemen, I'm going to show you something beautiful." Apparently, there were no women in the class at that time. Stanciu says, "He proceeded to elegantly lay out several fundamental theorems about vector spaces. When finished, he stepped back from the blackboard and said, 'Isn't that beautiful.'" Apparently, one student didn't see it, but the rest of them did.

I want to tell you about another experience I had of beauty in physics. It was my senior year in high school. I was taking physics and calculus at the time. For some reason, I was reviewing some of the kinematics equations when I suddenly realized that a handful of them were actually the same equation with calculus applied. If I took just one of those equations and performed a calculus operation called taking a derivative, I got another equation which could then be rearranged to form the definition of acceleration. When I made the same operation again, I got another one of the kinematics equations. They were all the same thing. There was a natural, inherent link between them all. And my mind was blown.

Another personal story I can share about an experience of beauty actually has to do with my study of philosophy, specifically the philosophy of Thomas Aquinas. I can't go into all of the details now, but Aquinas' understanding of Being illuminates and links everything else. All of reality suddenly made more sense to me. Physics gave an elegant and succinct description of the physical world, but Aquinas' philosophy went all the way to the Foundation of the existence of things.

This next story of an experience with beauty in mathematics is particularly impressive to me because I found it, not while reading a book about physics or math, but in a book about Ancient Greece written by a historian. H.D.F. Kitto in his book *The Greeks* tries to convey to the reader the excitement and attitude of the Pythagoreans towards mathematics. In order to get the idea across, Kitto tells his own story of mathematical discovery. He says that for some reason he started thinking about what the relationship would be between the square of a number and the product of its adjacent numbers. For example, the square of 10 is 100, and the product of its neighbors, 9 and 11, is 99, one less than 100. He then wondered if the "one less" pattern would hold, so he tried it with different numbers and found that the pattern worked. He says that "with growing excitement" he then algebraically proved the "one less" relationship. This is gratifying and impressive to me, that a historian still has the ability to prove something algebraically.

His excitement continued as he thought about the product of the numbers that were two away from the squared number. 8 x 12 = 96, three less than 99, the product of 9 and 11. He says, "It was with great delight that I disclosed to myself a whole system of numerical behavior of which my mathematical teachers had left me (I am glad to say) in complete ignorance." He found that if he moved out one more, for example to 7 and 13, he got five less than 96. As he went further and further out, the differences between each product formed the odd number series. Then, even more amazing to him, was the fact that, if each product were subtracted from the original 100, he got the pattern 1, 4, 9, 16.... He goes on, "They had never told me, and I had never suspected, that Numbers play these grave and beautiful games with each other, from everlasting to everlasting, independently (apparently) of time, space and the human mind. It was an impressive peep into a new and perfect universe." So even this historian can have an experience of the beauty of mathematics in some relatively simple arithmetic and algebra and the patterns that are produced. His teacher may not have shown him that particular instance of beauty, but they had at least prepared him to be able to see the beauty when he later had the time and inspiration to discover it.

What I am going to do now is go through a bunch of quotes about beauty. As you can tell from your time in my class and from looking at my walls, I have collected a lot of quotes, and that I really like sharing them. Most of these quotes are from the wall, and they have to do with beauty in math and science, but that is primarily because those are a lot of the books I have read, and it is from those books that I have synthesized these thoughts. I am trying to show you that I am not alone in my thoughts on this, and I am going to appeal to people who speak with more authority, experience and eloquence in these areas.

So, to start, here is a quote from Roger Penrose, a mathematician and theoretical physicist. He was one of Stephen Hawking's professors. He says, "A beautiful idea has a much greater chance of being a correct idea than an ugly one." There is a link between beauty and truth, even in science. Physicists often appeal to beauty as an important indicator of the truth of a theory. Again, he says, "Aesthetic criteria are enormously valuable in forming our judgments." We often think that physics is cold and hard, all about pure logic and agreement with experiment. Not at all. Besides the fact that humans are involved, beauty plays an important role, as Penrose says.

This quote is from a poet, Edna St. Vincent Millay, who is not a mathematician or physicist, and the quote is a line in a poem. "Euclid alone has looked on Beauty bare." I can't say I agree one hundred percent with this, but it has a point. There is a purity to the beauty of geometry. Remember, Euclid wrote the first textbook on geometry and is credited with compiling and synthesizing it.

Again, about the beauty that physicists look for in theories, here is a quote from Brian Greene, a theoretical physicist. This quote is from a book called *The Elegant Universe*, so he appeals to beauty in the name of the book! He has written other books and he even had a TV show at one time. "It is certainly the case that some decisions made by theoretical physicists are founded upon an aesthetic sense, a sense of which theories have an elegance and beauty of structure on par with the world we experience." Elegance. Beauty. It's all over the place!

The link between physics and mathematics has been a subject of fascination for many scholars. In fact, there was a famous essay published in the 1960s in a mathematics journal entitled "On the Unreasonable Effectiveness of Mathematics in the Physical Sciences" by Eugene Wigner. Why is math so perfect for expressing physics? We don't know. It doesn't have to work that way. But it does. It is mind-blowing. Physicist Kenneth Ford writes, "Physicists stand in awe of the power of mathematics to describe Nature." Historian of philosophy Etienne Gilson writes, "Mathematics provides science with its most perfect form of expression."

The German poet and philosopher, Goethe, said, "Geometry is frozen music." He is saying that the beauty that we experience and love in music would look like geometry if we could somehow freeze it and see it. The philosopher and mathematician, and co-inventor of calculus, Gottfried Wilhelm Leibniz wrote, "The pleasure we experience from music comes from counting, but counting unconsciously. Music is nothing but unconscious arithmetic." This is another quote that I don't think it completely correct, but Leibniz again sees the connection between music and mathematics.

Now, I have a lot of quotes from Stephen Barr. He is a theoretical particle physicist at University of Delaware. Regarding mathematics, he says, "The first thing to appreciate is that mathematics is not just a collection of facts. Rather, what makes mathematics so interesting – at least to some people – is the fact that one can start with a few obvious and seemingly trivial statements and deduce from them a large number of things that are not at all obvious or trivial." Remember the simplicity of beauty. Everything is related. Then the brilliance, all of the many things that are illuminated. That is what Barr is talking about here, those aspects of beauty in math.

Regarding the harmony, Barr says, "As one goes deeper into the working of the physical world, to more and more fundamental levels of the laws of nature, one encounters not ever less structure and symmetry but ever more. The deeper one goes the more orderly nature looks, the more subtle and intricate its designs." "Science has given us new eyes that allow us to see down to the deeper roots of the world's structure, and there *all* we see is order and symmetry of pristine mathematical purity." Harmony, symmetry, balance. At the fundamental level of the material universe, that is all there is. Again, Barr says, "What science has shown us is that most of the beauty and order in nature is hidden from our eyes."

The famous mathematician Henri Poincare said, "Without a rather high degree of aesthetic instinct no man will ever be a great mathematical discoverer." He is saying that the ability to be a great mathematician depends on having the ability to recognize beauty.

Jacques Hadamard was a mathematician and psychologist. He wrote a book entitled *The Psychology of Invention in the Mathematical Field*. He comments on what Poincare said. "With Poincare, we see something else, the intervention of the sense of beauty playing its part as an indispensable means of finding. We have reached the double conclusion: that invention is choice and that this choice is imperatively governed by the sense of scientific beauty."

Ok. Hopefully by now you are convinced that there is such a thing as the beauty I have been talking about and that it plays an important role in mathematics and science. Great. Who cares? Why think about beauty or take the time to learn about it? Is it really so important to be able to recognize it?

First of all, beauty is a pointing finger to truth, and truth is the ultimate good of the human mind. One of the names for beauty is "the splendor of truth." Beauty is the shiny-ness of truth. Again, a quote from one of the founders of modern physics, Paul Dirac: "It is more important for the scientist to have beautiful equations than agreement with experiment." That is a shocking statement! But it agrees with what others have said. Beauty is important because it is an indicator of truth. Richard Feynman, another great physicist from the 20th century said, "You can recognize truth by its beauty and simplicity."

However, there is another reason. Beauty is a good in itself. Some things are good because they get us something else. Some things are good in themselves. Beauty is one of those things. Somehow, we as humans seem to need beauty. The desire for beauty is part of our nature. Peter Kreeft, a philosophy professor at Boston College, whom I have had the pleasure of meeting and auditing a couple of classes from, wrote a book – he wrote *a lot* of books – about the philosophy of J.R.R. Tolkien, author of *The Lord of the Rings*. Kreeft's book would be a great introduction to philosophy in general, especially if you are a Tolkien fan. In that book, Kreeft writes, "Every human soul craves 'the good, the true, and the beautiful' absolutely and without limit." Without beauty, we are incomplete.

And here is my last anecdote. Back to music again. You all know Handel's work called *The Messiah* because the choir sings the Hallelujah chorus at every winter concert. That song is from *The Messiah* by Handel. When he first wrote and performed the piece, Handel went to his friend's house a few days later, and his friend congratulated him on the "noble entertainment" he had provided for the people of London. Handel was offended. He said, "My Lord, I should be sorry if I only entertained them; I wish to make them better." Handel knew that beauty ennobles us and makes us more of who we are.

So, that's it. It has been a privilege to have you all in class this year. Have a great summer and keep in touch!

# Appendix: the Quotes

I have a collection of quotes that I put up on my wall. I am always adding and taking away quotes, and I am not sure how many of them are actually read by my students (especially the longer ones that are so small from far away). I don't necessarily agree wholeheartedly with every quote, but I think there is an important element of wisdom in all of them.

A few of the quotes are in a special language called math. A good quote is one that states a profound idea succinctly and elegantly, and the math statements do just that, only in a language unlike the other quotes. I have them on the wall because I think they are beautiful.

## *Math and Physics*

The symmetries and patterns found at one level are manifestations of greater symmetries and more comprehensive patterns lying concealed at the more fundamental levels. – Stephen Barr

The pleasure we experience from music comes from counting, but counting unconsciously. Music is nothing but unconscious arithmetic. - G. W. Leibniz

Geometry is frozen music. –Goethe

Rather than a problem to be solved, the world is a joyful mystery to be contemplated with gladness and praise. - Pope Francis

$$e^{i\pi}+1=0$$

φ [the Greek letter phi represents the Golden Ratio]

It is not at all natural that "laws of nature" exist, much less that man is able to discover them. -Eugene Wigner

Mathematics provides science with its most perfect form of expression. – Etienne Gilson

Euclid alone has looked on Beauty bare. - Edna St. Vincent Millay

Physicists stand in awe of the power of mathematics to describe Nature. - Kenneth W. Ford

In science, order comes from *greater* order. – Stephen Barr

What is it that breathes fire into the equations and make a universe for them to describe? - Stephen Hawking

They had never told me, and I had never suspected, that Numbers play these grave and beautiful games with each other, from everlasting to everlasting, independently (apparently) of time, space and the human mind. It was an impressive peep into a new and perfect universe. -H.D.F. Kitto

Science has given us new eyes that allow us to see down to the deeper roots of the world's structure, and there *all* we see is order and symmetry of pristine mathematical purity. – Stephen Barr

Where the genuine scientist is generally amazed at the meagerness of knowledge in his own field, the layman is apt to assign omniscience as what he takes to be a property of scientific transcendence. – Walker Percy

The world revealed to us by science is a world of wonder and glory, magic and mystery. -Roy Abraham Varghese

It is more important for the scientist to have beautiful equations than agreement with experience. – Paul Dirac

Joy in looking and comprehending is nature's most beautiful gift. - Albert Einstein

All the fifty years of conscious brooding have brought me no closer to the answer to the question, 'What are light quanta [photons]?' Of course today every rascal thinks he knows the answer, but he is deluding himself. –Albert Einstein

One had to lose one's common sense in order to perceive what was happening at the atomic level. – Richard Feynman

If your head doesn't swim when you think about the quantum, you haven't understood it. - Niels Bohr

The way we have to describe Nature is generally incomprehensible to us. – Richard Feynman

The Newtonian theory of gravitation, on its appearance, disturbed almost all investigators of nature because it was founded on an uncommon unintelligibility. Now it has become *common* unintelligibility. - Ernst Mach

[Gravity is] so great an absurdity that I believe no man who has in philosophical matters a competent faculty of thinking can ever fall into it. -Isaac Newton

No matter what you look at, if you look at it closely enough, you are involved in the entire universe. –Richard Feynman

Take the observations of supernovae and the cosmic microwave background, apply the other cornerstone of twentieth-century physics, quantum theory, and you got gibberish. -Richard Panek

$$F_G = \frac{m_1 m_2}{r^2}$$

For most, the motion of the earth is more than a matter of faith; it is a matter of unconscious faith. –Anthony Rizzi

Men love to wonder, and that is the seed of science. - Ralph Waldo Emerson

[Quantum mechanics] describes nature as absurd from the point of view of common sense. And it fully agrees with experiment. So I hope you can accept nature as She is – absurd. – Richard Feynman

Do not despair if a full understanding [of quantum mechanics] proves elusive. It is the nature of the subject itself. – Roger Penrose

As one goes deeper and deeper into the workings of the physical world, to more and more fundamental levels of the laws of nature, one encounters not ever less structure and symmetry but ever more. The deeper one goes the more orderly nature looks, the more subtle and intricate its designs. – Stephen Barr

A beautiful idea has a much greater chance of being a correct idea than an ugly one. - Roger Penrose

Aesthetic criteria are enormously valuable in forming our judgments. – Roger Penrose
It is certainly the case that some decisions made by theoretical physicists are founded upon an aesthetic sense- a sense of which theories have an elegance and beauty of structure on par with the world we experience. - Brian Greene

The universe is such a wonderfully rich and complex place that the discovery of the final theory, in the sense we are describing here, would not spell the end of science. - Brian Greene

What science has shown us is that most of the beauty and order in nature is hidden from our eyes. – Stephen Barr

We have an unscientific attitude toward science. There is no scientific proof that only scientific proofs are good proofs; no way to prove by the scientific method that the scientific method is the only valid method. -Peter Kreeft

The real wonder is not that the Cosmos is now seen as wonderful but that it is not. Despite its inconceivable vastness, it is seen not as wonderful but as something that can be explained. – Walker Percy

## *On Reading*

It is better to spend time with dead people who bring you to life than with live people who lead you to death. –Matthew Kelly

Well-reasoned thoughts, conveyed with well-chosen words, can touch us as deeply as a moving symphony or a driving drum beat. -Eric Bronson

Students who read Plato, Aristotle, St. Paul, and St. Augustine often are struck to find themselves brought more up-to-date, in a way, than when they read the *New York Times* or the latest textbook. The former sources possess a freedom and an intelligence that the latter somehow lack. - James Schall

The important thing about a book is to know what is says. It is a living path to an author who is not here, who may in fact have lived centuries earlier, but who can still teach us. - James Schall

Somebody who reads only newspapers and at best books of contemporary authors looks to me like an extremely nearsighted person who scorns eyeglasses. He is completely dependent on the prejudices and fashions of his times, since he never gets to see or hear anything else. And what a person thinks on his own without being stimulated by the thoughts and experiences of other people is even in the best case rather paltry and monotonous. - Albert Einstein

To know a single old book well, even if it hasn't been canonized as a "classic," is to have a certain anchorage you can't get from most contemporary writing. -Joseph Sobran

Books really do change our lives, because what we read today walks and talks with us tomorrow. – Matthew Kelly

Employ your time in improving yourself by other men's writings, so that you shall gain easily what others have labored hard for. - Socrates

Tell me what you read and I will tell you what you are. - James Schall

Thought determines action, and one of the most powerful influences on thought is the material we choose to read. – Matthew Kelly

Most books, especially in philosophy and especially in modern times, are strong on figuring and weak on seeing. -Peter Kreeft
When you internalize an author whose vision or philosophy is both rich and out of fashion, you gain a certain immunity from the pressures of the contemporary. -Joseph Sobran

## *Mind and Mankind*

We do not infer the existence *of* our minds, rather we infer the existence of everything else *with* our minds. - Stephen Barr

Thought determines action. –Matthew Kelly

To lose the capacity of wonder is, in fact, to lose our greatest avenue of knowledge, for the most important truths can be known only if we have a minimal comprehension of their grandeur. -Roy Abraham Varghese

I think, therefore I am. – Rene Descartes

Man by nature desires to know. – Aristotle

It is better to be a human being dissatisfied than a pig satisfied. It is better to be Socrates dissatisfied than a fool satisfied. - J.S. Mill

A knowing being lives most acutely, most vividly, when it thinks about *what is*. - James Schall

The quality of *understanding* is not something that can ever be encapsulated in a set of rules. - Roger Penrose

Our actions are determined by our last most dominant thought. – Matthew Kelly

Spoken words are a sign of what occurs in the soul. - Thomas
Aquinas

What you allow to occupy your mind forms the reality of your
life. —Matthew Kelly

He who stands for nothing falls for everything. - Alexander
Hamilton

Of all the billions and billions of strange objects in the Cosmos
– novas, quasars, pulsars, black holes – you are beyond doubt
the strangest. – Walker Percy

It is totally unfitting for a man to act as a beast, because that
means the complete oblivion of his own nature, and hence his
final destruction. -Etienne Gilson

Some drink at the fountain of knowledge...others just gargle.
-Anonymous

A mind that cannot or will not make an affirmation or
judgement is not a mind. -James Schall

Some people have something worth saying, but they never say
it. Others don't have anything worth saying, but they just keep
saying it. -Unknown

Do not conform to the patterns of this world. Be transformed
by the renewing of your mind. - Romans 12:2

Millions of mild black-coated men call themselves sane and
sensible merely because they always catch the fashionable
insanity, because they are hurried into madness after madness
by the maelstrom of the world. - G.K. Chesterton

We talk of wild animals; but man is the only wild animal. It is
man that has broken out. - G.K. Chesterton

ΓΝΩΘΙ ΣΕΑΥΤΟΝ  [Know Thyself]  -Inscribed above the door
of the Ancient Delphic Oracle
The most incomprehensible thing about the universe is that it
is comprehensible. - Albert Einstein

Man is distinguished from the rest of creation by his
intelligence and his freedom. -Thomas Merton

The very summit of man's attainment is the capacity to marvel.
– Eckermann

You live in a deranged age – more deranged than usual,
because despite great scientific and technological advances,
man has not the faintest idea of who he is or what he is doing.
– Walker Percy

## *Philosophy and Wisdom*

There resides in every man a natural desire to know the
cause of any effect which he sees; and thence arises wonder
in men. –Thomas Aquinas

It cannot be too often repeated that philosophy is
everybody's business. To be a human being is to be
endowed with the proclivity to philosophize. - Mortimer
Adler

Herein is the evil of ignorance, that he who is neither good
nor wise is nevertheless satisfied with himself. -Socrates

Philosophy is not confined to philosophers. Everyone has a
philosophy. -Peter Kreeft

Wisdom and speakers of wisdom are in rather short supply
in our civilization. What we have instead are the experts. -
Sheldon Vanauken

The highest felicity in us consists in understanding the highest intelligible. – Thomas Aquinas

Knowledge is its own purpose, an end in itself, that it is good to know. - James Schall

There is no worse metaphysics than disguised metaphysics. – Jacques Maritain

One can no more philosophize with non-philosophical instruments than paint with a flute or a piano. – Jacques Maritain

If you look closely enough at anything, you will see that there is nothing more exciting than truth. -Richard Feynman

Each life is its own philosophical adventure aimed at finding the truth and living it. -James Schall

Save us from the young men and women, or the old ones for that matter, who are never unsettled in their souls about *what is*, about reality's meaning. - James Schall

It is by our philosophy that we see the world, not by our eyes, unless our eyes themselves are directed by a philosophy that affirms *what is*. - James Schall

Each must discover in his own soul this longing to know. - James Schall

The beginning of philosophy is wonder. – Josef Pieper

The real discovery is not that we have questions, but that we have answers to such questions. Our minds cannot be satisfied with mere questioning, even though to question is to start to seek an answer. - James Schall

There are two kinds of people in the world: the fools who think that they are wise and the wise who know that they are fools. – Peter Kreeft

Wherever the truth of our judgments, opinions, or beliefs is a proper concern, we should be prepared to argue with those who disagree with us, with the firm hope that our disagreement can be resolved. –Mortimer Adler

The ultimate beatitude of man consists in the use of his highest function, which is the operation of his intellect. – Thomas Aquinas

The life of the mind is ultimately concerned with truth. - James Schall

Above all we must seek truth, for a meaning or a happiness or a fulfillment which is not grounded in truth is worthless. -Stephen D. Schwarz

Be careful not to be so open-minded that your brains fall out. – G.K. Chesterton

Better to believe a painful truth than a comforting illusion. -Stephen D. Schwarz

Man, by all his proper operations fittingly ordered and rightly directed, strives to attain the contemplation of truth. -Thomas Aquinas

Just as the suitors of Penelope consorted with her maid-servants when they were not able to approach the queen herself, so also do those who are not able to approach true wisdom wear themselves thin over the other kinds of education which have no value. -Bion

What is liberty without wisdom, and without virtue? It is the greatest of all possible evils. -Edmund Burke

To wonder is to know and to know is to wonder. -Roy Abraham Varghese

There is no short road to riches in philosophy. -Etienne Gilson

To say of what is that it is or of what is not that it is not is true; to say of what is that it is not or of what is not that it is is false. - Aristotle

A small error in principle is a large error in conclusion. - Reginald Garrigou-Lagrange

Were it in my power to do so, I would rather leave you with a gift. Not wisdom, which I have not and no man can give, but the next best thing: the love of wisdom, for which philosophy is another word. -Etienne Gilson

Without wonder, men and women would lapse into deadening routine and little by little would become incapable of a life which is genuinely personal. -St. John Paul II

If anyone imagines that he knows something, he does not yet know as he ought to know. -1 Corinthians 8:2

Keep hold of instruction, do not let go; guard her, for she is your life. -Proverbs 4:13

Wisdom is better than jewels, and all that you may desire cannot compare with her. -Proverbs 8:11

To get wisdom is better than gold; to get understanding is to be chosen rather than silver. -Proverbs 16:16
There is gold, and abundance of costly stones; but the lips of knowledge are a precious jewel. -Proverbs 20:15

Do not toil to acquire wealth; be wise enough to desist. - Proverbs 23:4

The beginning of wisdom is the most sincere desire for instruction. - Wisdom 6:17

If you see an intelligent man, visit him early; let your foot wear out his doorstep. - Sirach 6:36

The possession of truth is the ultimate good of the human mind. –Mortimer Adler

The really damaging thing about stupidity is its self-satisfaction. – Plato

Philosophy emerges as one of the noblest of human tasks. –St. John Paul II

When a matter of the intellect is settled it is not dead; rather it is immortal. -G.K. Chesterton

If you know only what *you* know, you don't even know that. You understand things only by contrast. -Peter Kreeft

Wonder is the origin of all philosophy. -Peter Kreeft

There are two ways to slide easily through life: to believe everything or to doubt everything. Both ways save us from thinking. - Alfred Korzybski

We ought to be alive enough to reality to see beauty all around us. Beauty is simply reality itself, perceived in a

special way that gives it a resplendent value of its own. -
Thomas Merton

Among all human pursuits, the pursuit of wisdom is more
perfect, more noble, more useful, and more full of joy. –
Thomas Aquinas

To be able to see something of the loftiest realities,
however thin and weak the sight may be, is a cause of the
greatest joy. – Thomas Aquinas

The unexamined life is not worth living.
- Socrates

The unexamined thought is not worth thinking. - Mortimer
Adler

Socrates frequently likens philosophy to music in its ability
to transform the souls of its listeners. -Eric Bronson

# *Teaching and Learning*

Whoever constitutes himself his own guide, becomes a disciple
of a fool. - Adolphe Tanquerey

No one, not even the best teacher, can help us to learn
anything unless we ourselves make the primary effort to learn
it. - Mortimer Adler

We are ultimately responsible for our own learning of what is
true. - James Schall

Only the proud cannot and will not be taught. -James Schall

The whole purpose of schooling or of the learning that we do in
school is to prepare us for the kind of learning that have to do
and ought to do for the rest of our lives. - Mortimer Adler

Only fools have no desire to become a little wiser. -Mortimer Adler

Falsehood and evil can be taught as easily as good. Education is a great power, but it can work either way. —Richard Feynman

Old men are always young enough to learn with profit. - Aeschylus

What's money if your mind is empty? Educate your mind! - Ruth McBride

Educate yourself or you'll be a nobody! -Ruth McBride

I cannot teach anybody anything, I can only make them think. — Socrates

One of the greatest problems of our time is that many are schooled but few are educated. - Thomas More

You can lead a boy to college, but you cannot make him think. - Elbert Hubbard

Only the educated are free. — Epictetus

The fragmentation of knowledge proves helpful for concrete applications, and yet it often leads to a loss of appreciation for the whole, for the relationships between things, and for the broader horizon, which then becomes irrelevant. - Pope Francis

You cannot teach a man anything; you can only help him find it within himself. - Galileo Galilei

A little knowledge that acts is worth infinitely more than much knowledge that is idle. - Khalil Gibran

Learning without thought is labor lost. Thought without learning is dangerous. - Confucius

Nurture your minds with great thoughts, for you will never go any higher than you think. - Benjamin Disraeli

If I have seen further than others it is because I have stood on the shoulders of giants. - Isaac Newton

We are like dwarfs seated on the shoulders of giants. We see more things than the Ancients and things more distant, but it is due neither to the sharpness of our sight nor the greatness of our stature, it is simply because they have lent us their own. - Bernard of Chartres

It is necessary for each generation to conserve the accomplishments of the past as a basis for making any advance to higher levels in the future. - Mortimer Adler

Learning is in itself good, and praiseworthy, and desirable. - Pope Leo XIII

It is necessary to call into council the views of our predecessors in order that we may profit from whatever is sound in their thought and avoid their errors. – Aristotle

There is no such thing as an uninteresting subject; the only thing that can exist is an uninterested person. – G.K. Chesterton

[Beethoven] made clear that "freedom" - imagination operating beyond constraints - and "progress" - a constant originality of achievement - were impossible without scholarship. - Edmund Morris

Of learning, as of virtue, it may be affirmed, that it is at once honoured and neglected. -Samuel Johnson

# *General Inspiration*

If you are going through hell, keep going. -Winston Churchill

The true value of a human being is determined primarily by the measure and the sense in which he has attained liberation from the self. - Albert Einstein

An inconvenience is only an adventure wrongly considered; and adventure is an inconvenience rightly considered. - G.K. Chesterton

A man who fails well is greater than one who succeeds badly. - Thomas Merton

Television commercials are educational. They teach you how stupid advertisers think you are. - Anonymous

People who cannot remember the past are condemned to repeat it. – George Santayana

Enjoying life is not the same as living a flourishing one. -Raja Halwani

Death falls heavy upon him who is too much known to others and too little to himself. –Seneca

He who boasts of his bravery in peace is but a short-sighted warrior. -Pope St. Gregory the Great

There are two kinds of people in the world: the proud who think that they are humble and the humble who know that they are proud. – Peter Kreeft

The only thing you can do easily is be wrong, and that is hardly worth the effort. -Norton Juster

A mystery is what cannot be seen, not because there is a barrier across our field of vision, but because the horizon is so far away. – Stephen Barr

That which is to be loved long must be loved with reason rather than with passion. -Samuel Johnson

We see a light, as it were, shining through all reality, something that incites us to respond to it, to behold it. There is a radiance to being. All things that are limited to themselves point to what is not themselves. -James Schall

Asking the right question is frequently more than halfway to the solution of the problem. - Werner Heisenberg

Light travels faster than sound. That's why some people appear bright until they speak. – Unknown

We move through life in such a distracted way that we do not even take the time and rest to wonder if any of the things we think, say, or do are *worth* thinking, saying or doing. -Henri Nouwen

The quality of a man matters more than his achievement. - H.D.F. Kitto

# About the Author

Matt D'Antuono is a high school physics teacher who lives in New Jersey with his beautiful wife and seven children.

He holds bachelor's degrees in physics and philosophy and a master's degree in special education.

He is working on a master's degree in philosophy at Holy Apostles in Cromwell, CT.

You can find him on YouTube at DonecRequiescat.

Made in the USA
Coppell, TX
18 July 2022